"Rex Houze's *Leadership Insights* is first-rate reading and packed with valuable insights. I especially benefited from Rex's thoughts on investing time wisely. Invest your time wisely and read this book."

  - Dean Lindsay, author of *Cracking the Networking CODE*

"Rex's positive mental attitude is contagious, and his leadership insights are right on the mark. If you believe, as I do, that leadership is more about the people and that leaders are defined and developed by those they lead, then you must read Rex's newest book, *Leadership Insights*."

  - R. Douglas Cowan

"Rex's focused approach and inclusive style enables everyone to relate to him and thus his message. We are a better company today, in part, due to his affiliation."

  - Fred Johnson, Davey Tree

"Rex's coaching tips are great! They are inspiring to read, and they get me to re-think my daily work activities. They also get me to re-focus on my goals each time I read them."

  - Mike Fernandes, President, Site Selection Services

"The coaching tips in *Leadership Insights* have been invaluable to both myself and the members of our team. They are uplifting, motivating, encouraging, and inspiring ... yet surprisingly simple to put into practice. We have found that these tips help make the entire team more motivated and productive."

  - Kathleen Victor, VP of Sales & Marketing, MarkerNET, Inc.

"Rex's management coaching has been very helpful in my career development. The topics he introduces and the techniques he offers have given me confidence in my leadership roles, as well as skills to be an effective member of any team."

  - Ian Scott, Project Developer, Davey Resource Group

"Rex's insights are inspirational, focused, and full of wisdom."

"Rex's coaching tips are applicable to every walk of life- they speak to the CEO of a powerhouse company, to an athlete, to a factory worker."

"I have always found Rex's writing and coaching to be both inspirational and straightforward. His ability to refocus energy on the things that matter has been invaluable, and his positive approach to problem solving is refreshing."

"Rex Houze motivates the motivator! His field-tested ideas have always given me and my clients practical tips that have improved our performance."

"This book, *Leadership Insights*, is a compilation of some of Rex's best insights and experiences. Every leader will benefit from the ideas and inspiration. You will not only want a copy for yourself, but for everyone on your team."

"Rex is a great writer, terrific platform speaker, and outstanding coach and motivator. He has the ability to simplify complex issues and support development of practical action plans that deliver results."

"Rex's books, coaching, and speaking are gifts to those seeking the next level of excellence in their career. Take advantage of them and spread the word about his works!"

"I have known and worked with Rex Houze for over 25 years. He is always there when you need him, and his advice has certainly stood the test of time."

- John Potts, CFP, RFC, Signature Planning, Inc.

"I have known and been influenced by Rex and his coaching for over 25 years. He has a "system" that, if conscientiously followed, will enable people to substantially improve in every area of their life."

- Michael D. Arabe

"When any leader implements these meaningful ideas, their people and business are bound to improve."

- Jerry S. Siegel, President, JASB Management Inc.

"In today's environment where everyone knows the importance of leadership, it is not always easy to get the point across. I have found Rex's unique way of concisely developing an approach that works very helpful."

- John Divine, The Leadership Group

"Thought provoking, challenging, and concise are just a few of the words I think of in regards to *Leadership Insights* and Rex Houze. Rex's insights on personal development are timely and timeless."

- Janell Gilman, Director of Communications & Events, Curves International

"Rex and his coaching insights are...'SIMPLY THE BEST'!"

- Paul Feld, PES, Inc.

"Rex's coaching tips have been a constant inspiration to me and have helped me stay on course in starting up two new companies."

- Mark Kapelinski, President/Owner, Midwest Commercial Developers, LLC, Dog Beds & Crates etc.

Leadership
Insights

This edition published by Rex Houze

First Edition 2008

ISBN 978-0-9791108-2-5

Layout by AT Impact Consulting, LLC, Dallas, Texas
Cover design by Alicia Drury, Rochester, NY
Printed by Signature Book Printing, Gaithersburg, MD

This book is dedicated to George T. Miedl, Ph.D., a high school teacher who made learning fun which set me on a lifetime journey of continuous learning.

George helped me find my direction early in life, believed in me, cared about me, and has continued to encourage me for over 50 years. I have gained a lot of insight about true leadership and friendship from his example.

CONTENTS

PREFACE

It was the summer of 1965, and I had just been recruited to join the Tallmadge, Ohio, Jaycees*. They were scheduled to compete in an upcoming flag football game and were in need of a quarterback. The famed "Toilet Bowl" was against their archrival, the Stow Jaycees. I was 24 at the time and completely unaware of the "ripple effect" this one decision would have on the rest of my life. **Little things can make a big difference.**

The team and organization displayed a great deal of camaraderie, and I was encouraged to attend meetings, get involved in community projects, and learn the Jaycee Creed, which was proudly displayed and recited at every meeting:

> "We believe:
> That faith in God gives meaning and purpose to human life;
> That the brotherhood of man transcends the sovereignty of nations;
> That government should be of laws rather than of men;
> That earth's great treasure lies in human personality;
> And that service to humanity is the best work of life."
> - C. William Brownfield

I recited this creed hundreds of times over the next 10 years. These 52 words have influenced my life in so many ways. **A few words can make a big difference.**

A few years later, in May of 1968, I was elected president of our local Jaycee chapter, which unfortunately was lacking leadership at the time. Although excited by the opportunity, the first few months of my presidency proved very difficult. We were struggling to accomplish our mission of "leadership development through community service" and were unable to make the impact in the

*The Jaycees is an International organization that was founded to provide leadership development through community service.

community that we wanted.

Then, in early August, I received a packet from the U.S. Jaycees entitled "Leadership in Action." It was a small booklet authored by Paul J. Meyer of SMI/LMI in Waco, TX. The booklet contained six chapters and was to be presented to the members of our local chapter.

John Foresman, a training specialist from Goodyear and a long time member of our chapter, agreed to facilitate the program. The material was first presented to our board members and then to our regular members. As a result, our local chapter caught "on fire." By the end of the year, we had doubled our membership and won several state awards. *A little booklet can make a big difference.*

In addition to its tremendous impact on our local Jaycee chapter, this small booklet had a significant effect on me and my career. During the "Leadership in Action" program, I discovered my passion for personal development and began setting numerous goals in every area of my life.

One of my most compelling goals during this time was to be elected president of the Ohio Jaycees.

Three years later, I achieved my goal and was elected the 42nd president of the Ohio Jaycees in a landslide victory over two other candidates. At age 29, I was the youngest person elected to this position in the history of this organization. *Written and specific goals can make a big difference.*

As the newly elected state president, I was responsible for 300 chapters and 15,000 members. Our executive committee was comprised of 13 individuals, and we had 67 people on our Board of Trustees. Although the demands associated with this position were equivalent to running a large business, I managed to visit nearly all of the 300 chapters while continuing to hold down a full-time job. Little did I know what great preparation this was for what was to follow in the future.

Throughout my Jaycee career, I learned a lot about relationship building, communication, bringing out the best in people, motivation, opening closed minds, and numerous other leadership techniques. I was also fortunate to meet a lot of great people who are a part of who I am today.

My experience as the president of the Ohio Jaycees was a tremendous honor and made a big difference in my life and my career. *One experience can make a big difference.*

Toward the end of my Jaycee career, I shared the podium with another speaker at a meeting in Cincinnati. After hearing my speech and delivering his own, the presenter called me back up to the podium. He presented me with a book by William Danforth entitled *I Dare You* and challenged me to use my speaking ability to bring out the best in people. Intrigued and invigorated by his challenge and the book, I stayed up reading until 2:00am when I finished the book. Although we had just met that evening, this particular individual influenced my career path. *One person can make a big difference.*

A few weeks later, in March of 1972, I was contacted by Jon Spelman, a director of franchise sales for LMI in Waco, TX. Jon wanted to know if I was interested in using what I had learned during my Jaycee career to turn my avocation into a vocation.

After careful thought and deliberation, I made a commitment and used our life savings to buy a franchise. Several weeks later, I opened my own business with no customers and no promise of income. *Commitment can make a big difference.*

With a strong desire to succeed, I hired a business coach who immediately encouraged me to establish goals in every area of my life. One of my most aggressive goals was to read one personal or business development book every week. Although it took several months to turn this goal into a habit, it was a lot easier once it became a habit. I have been true to this goal for over 30 years now and continue to read more than 50 personal, leadership, and business development books every year. *Learning can make a big difference.*

As I grew as an individual, my business grew as well. Over the next 28 years, I recruited and developed a team of business coaches, coached independent business owners, wrote several programs, books, booklets, and modules, conducted hundreds of training sessions, facilitated a multitude of leadership development programs, and delivered hundreds of speeches on various leadership topics. *All of these experiences, one event at a time, made a big difference.*

Since my "Leadership in Action" experience in 1968, I have had a passion to help people bring out the best in themselves and others and have spent my career making a difference in the lives of others.

My goal with *Leadership Insights* is to provide you with a series of unique insights that will help you bring out the best in yourself and those around you. *Each insight included within this book can make a big difference. However, several insights, added together, can make a huge difference.*

GO FORTH AND MAKE A DIFFERENCE!

HOW TO USE THIS BOOK

Every day is an opportunity to advance both personally and professionally. As an individual, it is up to you to decide how you will approach each day and in what ways, if any, you will choose to make a difference. J. Martin Kohe, in his book *Your Greatest Power*, wrote that our greatest power is the power to choose. Thank you for choosing to read this book.

Leadership Insights is a personal and professional development tool which, when used, will enable you to stimulate change, hone your skills, and ultimately make a difference by becoming a positive influence in your life and in the lives of those around you. I believe that insight precedes change and without change there will be no improvement. This book is designed to give you insight, as well as the motivation to make the changes necessary to improve your performance and results.

Throughout this book, you will be given the opportunity to make a personal commitment to change by assessing your current performance and establishing new goals. To achieve maximum performance and optimal results, I encourage you to invest the time to write your responses at the end of the designated chapters. Doing so will enable you to establish written goals and drastically increase your probability of enjoying more success.

Writing crystallizes thought and crystallized thought motivates action. Your goal-directed, motivated action will pay big dividends in improved performance and results. Thank you for reading this book and taking the appropriate action. Best wishes for a successful journey toward bringing out the best in yourself and others.

1

MANAGEMENT RESOLUTIONS
FOR THE NEW YEAR - I

THROUGHOUT THE NEW YEAR I WILL:

1. Recognize that I am responsible for achieving results through others and that I need them more than they need me.

2. Be profitable and productive by improving utilization of personnel, material and other assets.

3. Develop our team based on personal accountability, i.e. each team member will deliver value greater than his or her total cost of employment.

4. Concentrate on excellence rather than perfection.

5. Become credible by earning my authority, not demanding it.

6. Use more influence and persuasion and less authority and control.

7. Ask better questions to get better answers and results.

8. Identify and stay in high payoff activities; and, get my team members to do the same.

9. Improve my ability to delegate and delegate more effectively.

10. Include people in the decision-making process to increase their commitment, ownership, and results.

11. Use positive confronting to correct inappropriate

behavior and I will resist the temptation to use sarcasm, criticism, or any other form of mental abuse.

12. Invest at least as much time on preventing problems as I spend solving them.

13. Hire for talent, train for skills, teach for knowledge, and motivate for growth and profit.

14. Focus on strengths and manage around weaknesses.

15. Develop a high sense of urgency for outcomes; and, at the same time, I will also be patient with people.

HAPPY PRODUCTIVE & PROFITABLE NEW YEAR!

••

I will focus on these resolutions until I turn each one into a habit:

1.

2.

3.

Then, I'll work on the next three.

2

PERSONAL GOALS STIMULATOR

If you are a relatively new goal setter, the following thought stimulators will help you identify goals that will be important to your success and happiness. If you are an experienced goal setter, these thought stimulators will help you expand your existing goals program. Either way, feel free to add your own stimulators.

- What do you want more of?
- What do you want less of?
- What do you want to improve?
- Where do you want to go?
- What do you want to do?
- What do you want to learn?
- Who would you like to meet?
- What position would you like to hold?
- What would you like to own?
- What are your family goals?
- What are your financial goals?
- What are your mental goals?
- What are your physical goals?
- What are your social goals?
- What are your spiritual goals?
- What are your professional goals?
- What are your personal development goals?
- What are your earning goals?
- What are your savings goals?

- What are your investment goals?
- What are your business goals?
- Who would you like to help/serve?
- What kind of lifestyle do you want?
- What debts would you like to pay off?
- What do you want to do for your children?
- What do you want to do for your siblings?
- What habits would you like to develop?
- What would you like to do for recreation?
- What kind of vacations would you like to take?
- What kind of relationships do you want?
- What skills would you like to develop?
- What would you like to do for your community?
- What is your passion?
- How much would you like to weigh?
- How much money would you like to earn?
- What specific habits would you like to develop?
- What specific habits would you like to change?
- What kind of home would you like to own?
- What improvements would you like to make in your current home?
- What new hobby would you like to begin?
- What pressures, stresses, or worries would you like to eliminate?
- What civic activities would you like to get involved in?
- What organizations would you like to join?

- ◆ What spiritual qualities would you like to develop?

- ◆ In what ways would you like to improve communication with family members?

- ◆ In what ways would you like to improve communication with business associates?

- ◆ If you had three unlimited wishes, what would you wish for?

"THE SADDEST WORDS OF TONGUE OR PEN ARE THESE...IT MIGHT HAVE BEEN."
- JOHN G. WHITTIER

....

My most important goals are:

1.

2.

3.

4.

5.

3
GOAL SETTING PRINCIPLES
AND HOW TO APPLY THEM

GOALS NEED TO…

Be WRITTEN. Writing crystallizes thought and crystallized thought motivates action. Also, a short pencil is better than a long memory. You can refer to written goals, communicate them, and create a front-of-the-mind awareness.

Be SPECIFIC. The mind can focus on the concrete better than it can the abstract.

Be PERSONAL. You are more likely to take action on your own goals than someone else's goals. When setting business goals, make sure you tie your "ownership" to each goal.

Be POSITIVE. Set goals on what you want to happen rather than what you don't want. Focus on growth rather than just survival; retention rather than turnover; quality rather than defects; and safety rather than accidents.

Be MEASURABLE and contain a METHOD FOR KEEPING SCORE. Imagine that your goals are a sporting event. What will you put on the scoreboard during the contest or in the box scores the next day?

Be TANGIBLE and INTANGIBLE. Whenever possible tie a tangible goal to each of your intangible goals and an intangible goal to each of your tangible goals. For example, if your tangible goal is to increase sales and/or profit by a specific amount, your supporting intangible goal might be to become a better coach so your people will perform better. The intangible goal to be a better coach can be supported by tangible goals that let you know that you are a better coach – for example, giving more positive feedback and less criticism or negative feedback.

Be LONG-RANGE and SHORT-RANGE. Long-range goals give you direction and purpose. Short-range goals provide motivation and are steps toward long-range goals.

Have SOME STRETCH. If goals are too easy, they won't motivate you and you may get bored. If goals are too difficult, they could cause stress and discouragement. Your reach should exceed your grasp for optimum motivation.

Contain ACTION STEPS. Action steps become short-range or bite-sized goals and create motivation and momentum. The completion of each action step can be cause for celebration.

Have a TIMETABLE, including DEADLINES. Deadlines increase focus, concentration, and stick-to-it-tiveness. Use them to your advantage.

....

Goals need to be S.M.A.R.T.
- *Specific and written*
- *Measurable*
- *Action-oriented*
- *Realistic*
- *Target date*

4

THOUGHTS ON COMMUNICATION

1. "Nothing in life is more important than the ability to communicate."

    - Gerald Ford

2. Communication is the glue that holds relationships together. It is the chief means by which people relate to one another.

3. Communication, like nature, abhors a vacuum. In the absence of communication, people will create their own messages, typically in the form of rumor, innuendo, and gossip.

4. "The void created by the failure to communicate is soon filled with poison, drivel, and misrepresentation."

    - C. Northcote Parkinson

5. Unfortunately, people get used to poor communication and accept it as a natural part of life.

6. Most, if not all, people think they are better communicators than they really are.

7. The biggest miscommunication is to assume communication has taken place.

8. When communication is done correctly, people will be inspired to follow, and in the process will achieve inspired results for themselves, for the leader, and for the organization.

9. Most conflicts and controversies are caused by people not understanding one another.

10. The moment people see that they are being understood,

they become motivated to understand your point of view.

11. Everybody wants to feel important. Everybody can feel important when somebody understands and believes them. It doesn't take much effort to help people feel important. Little things, done deliberately, at the right time, can make a big difference.

12. "Wisdom is the reward you get for a lifetime of listening when you'd have preferred to talk."
    - Doug Larson

13. "One of the best ways to persuade others is with your ears - by listening to them."
    - Dean Rusk

14. The answers are in the questions.

15. "People's opinions, thoughts, and desires are often molded by the questions they are asked."
    - Kevin Hogan

16. "I'd rather know some of the questions than all of the answers."
    - James Thurber

17. When you talk you only say something that you already know. When you listen, you learn what someone else knows.

18. One of the key principles of business management is that words of encouragement or discouragement affect production. Leaders have great power to encourage and build up or destroy, discourage, and debilitate their followers with words.

19. If you want to change what people are doing, you have

to change what they are thinking. To change what they are thinking, you have to change what you are saying and, perhaps, how you are saying it.

....

The thought that resonates with me at this time is number _____ and here's why:

Action I will take as a result of this thought:

5
THOUGHTS ON MOTIVATION

1. People do things for their reasons, not ours. Find out what they want and why they want it.

2. All motivation is self-motivation. Before you can motivate someone else, you need to motivate yourself.

3. People do things to gain a benefit or avoid a loss. People won't change their behavior unless it makes a difference to them to do so. Common motivators are: Pride, Profit, Pleasure, and Protection (pain avoidance).

4. "The strongest human force for motivation is goal setting."
    - Paul J. Meyer

5. Attitude is everything; it impacts everything you do. It determines your performance.

6. "When your attitude improves, so do your circumstances."
    - Keith Harrell

7. "We are where we are, and what we are, because of the dominating thoughts that occupy our mind."
    - W. Clement Stone

8. Try agreeing with people instead of disagreeing with them. See how right you can make others instead of how wrong.

9. "Motivation is what gets you started. Habit is what keeps you going."
    - Jim Ryun

10. "When people believe in themselves, it is amazing

what they can accomplish."

- Sam Walton

11. "People will sit up and take notice of you when you sit up and take notice of what makes them sit up and take notice."

- Frank Romer

12. "Know your people; know their goals; know their activity; know their results."

- Rex Houze

13. "Ability is what you're capable of doing. Motivation determines what you do. Attitude determines how well you do it."

- Lou Holtz

14. "Honest criticism is hard to take, particularly from a relative, a friend, an acquaintance or a stranger."

- Franklin P. Jones

15. "Recognition is an energizing action which can go up, down, and sideways. Just say, 'Thank you;' 'Good job;' 'You're the best;' and positive energy flows between, to, and from both people."

- Paula Gavin

16. "Treat people as though they were what they ought to be and you help them become what they are capable of being."

- Goethe

17. "The best way to inspire people to superior performance is to convince them by everything you do and your everyday attitude that you are wholeheartedly supporting them."

- Harold Geneen

18. "Don't wait until people do things exactly right before you praise them."

    - The One Minute Manager®

19. "Do not let what you cannot do interfere with what you can do."

    - John Wooden

20. People flourish with praise and acceptance and diminish with criticism and rejection.

....

The thought that resonates with me at this time is number _____ and here's why:

Action I will take as a result of this thought:

6

PERFORMANCE IMPROVEMENT PRINCIPLES

1. Feedback is the foundation of all relationships. It affects the way people think, feel, act, and react. The quality of relationships is dependant on the quantity and quality of the feedback.

2. Achievement requires continuous feedback.

3. People would rather be inspired than fixed or corrected.

4. In organizations real power and energy is generated through relationships.

5. "I absolutely believe that people, unless coached, never reach their maximum capabilities."

   - Bob Nardelli

6. Employees trade their performance for their coach's appreciation, approval, and applause.

7. Trust and communication are the two organizational problems listed most often by employee surveys. Any performance improvement program needs to address these two areas.

8. One of the most valuable additions to a person's life that a leader can provide is reassurance.

9. Where there's a lack of feedback, people will manufacture their own feedback, quite often based on their worst fears.

10. It discourages people when they have to guess where you're coming from every day.

11. When you ignore people (intentionally or unintentionally) they will think you are uncaring,

unconcerned, aloof, and/or arrogant.

12. Be alert for people whose questions aren't questions. They could be pleas for attention.

13. "There is nothing else that so kills the ambition of a person as criticism from superiors."
- Charles Schwab

14. "Abilities wither under criticism. They blossom under encouragement."
- Dale Carnegie

15. "There is no such thing as constructive criticism."
- Dale Carnegie

16. Negative criticism can cause: resentment, depression, anger and/or sabotage.

17. People will sabotage your leadership if they feel alienated and under-appreciated.

18. Without goals, people will just fight fires, work through emotional upsets, and worry about the dysfunctional behavior of other people.

IF YOU ARE A:	YOU'LL FIND:
Babysitter	Babies
Problem solver	Problems
Firefighter	Fires
Coach	Players

**REGARDLESS OF TITLE, YOUR JOB IS
PERFORMANCE IMPROVEMENT COACH**

••

One idea for improving my/our performance is:

7

COMMON TIMEWASTERS

How you invest your time will determine, to a large degree, the outcomes you enjoy. Listed below are some common timewasters that can keep people from accomplishing all they want. Check all the timewasters that might apply to you. Then, identify the top three. Work on these until you've overcome them, then continue the process until you are effectively using your time to achieve your goals.

- ❏ Attempting too much
- ❏ Procrastination; delaying distasteful tasks
- ❏ Indecision
- ❏ Unclear communication
- ❏ Perfectionism; too much attention to detail
- ❏ Preoccupation with problems
- ❏ Not actively listening
- ❏ Excessive socializing
- ❏ Lack of, or ineffective, delegation
- ❏ Constant checking on employees
- ❏ Inability to say "no"
- ❏ Unnecessary or unproductive meetings
- ❏ Allowing constant interruptions by others
- ❏ Insisting on knowing all and seeing all
- ❏ Assistant not aware of changes in schedule
- ❏ Allowing upward delegation
- ❏ Doing other people's work
- ❏ Not effectively training staff

- ❏ Firefighting (80% of "Crisis Management" events are preventable)
- ❏ Insufficient planning, scheduling, or organizing
- ❏ Relying on mental notes
- ❏ Not effectively utilizing waiting time and travel time
- ❏ Inefficient office layout
- ❏ Facts, phone numbers, and other vital information not at hand
- ❏ No daily plan
- ❏ No self-imposed deadlines
- ❏ No follow-up system
- ❏ Lack of procedures
- ❏ Not using prime time for priority items
- ❏ Spending time on low-priority items
- ❏ Lack of written goals or poorly defined goals
- ❏ Not enough "Quiet Time"
- ❏ _____
- ❏ _____

....

I will work on these three first:

1.

2.

3.

8

HOW PRODUCTIVE ARE YOU?

The areas listed in the High Value column below will help you be more productive and the areas listed in the Low Value column will get in the way of being productive. During any activity ask: "Is what I am doing right now leading me toward or away from my goals and helping me be more or less productive?"

High Value	Low Value
Quality time with direct reports	Criticizing employees
Quality time with customers	Frivolous conversations
Setting goals and planning	Bustling around without planning
Personal development reading	Responding to every interruption
Improving job knowledge	Complaining
Listening to educational CD's	Making excuses
Focusing on high payoff activities	Unproductive or unnecessary meetings
Maintaining a positive attitude	Thinking unproductive thoughts
Developing and practicing new skills	Blaming
Making and keeping commitments	Trying to remember unwritten commitments
Being and staying organized	Living with clutter

High Value	Low Value
Keeping score on a daily basis	Embracing fear and associated emotions
Giving quality feedback	Giving little or inappropriate feedback
Closing communication loops	Assuming communication has taken place
Delegating appropriate tasks	Trying to do everything yourself

Perfection is not the goal; excellence is. Improving how you use your time in order to be more productive will be crucial in your pursuit of excellence.

Invest a little time each day to assess how you are using your time. Then take action to eliminate low value activities and bolster the high value investments you make daily.

"Things that matter most should not be at the mercy of things which matter least."

- Johann Goethe

"Doing the right thing is more important than doing things right."

- Peter Drucker

....

Action I will take to be more productive:

9
MANAGE YOURSELF, NOT TIME

1. **Spend a lot of time in your primary areas of responsibility** - Resist the temptation to get distracted or drawn into low-payoff activities.

2. **Focus on improving in the areas that you spend a lot of time** - If you are currently spending four hours per week in a given activity, improving your effectiveness by 10 percent will give you an extra 20 hours per year that can be invested in other high-payoff areas.

3. **Invest as much time as possible in areas where you have the greatest strengths** - Working in areas of your greatest strengths is more pleasurable and boosts your energy rather than drains it.

4. **Stay in the moment** - Focus on where you are. The mind can only focus on one thing at a time. When you jump back and forth between multiple tasks or thoughts, you do not give either task or thought your full attention. When you do not give something your full attention, you will be less effective.

5. **Use synergy.** - Combine several objectives into one activity.

6. **Cut larger tasks into bite-sized chunks** - Large tasks can be overwhelming. When you break these tasks into bite-sized chunks – something you can do immediately, within the hour, or this week – you break inertia, overcome procrastination, and create momentum.

7. **Start and finish strong** - Ninety percent of failure can be attributed to not starting or quitting too soon. Getting off to a fast start gives you momentum, motivation, and

the confidence to continue. Finishing strong increases the likelihood of success.

8. **Divide and conquer** - Isolate tasks that need your undivided attention. Set up separate folders, electronic files, or notebooks as needed.

9. **Keep "Could Do" lists** - These are tasks or projects that you could do when you are blocked on your high-priority tasks or in downtime.

10. **Organize and categorize** - Keep things you use on a regular basis in close proximity to your desk. Set up and use a filing system that insures quick retrieval.

11. **Simplify** - Look for ways to cut out steps, group similar activities, or otherwise streamline processes. Set up systems that will optimize flow.

12. **Manage distractions** - Clear the clutter, both physical and mental. Close your door. Change location. Turn your computer monitor or close your laptop. Turn your phone to silent mode. Some additional techniques for managing distractions include having written goals, setting deadlines and target dates, making and keeping commitments, and maintaining your energy level.

....

Action I will take to manage myself better:

10
TRUST – THE GREAT ELIXIR

Trust is the single most important factor in personal relationships. Trust is the feeling that we can depend on another person. Management, or coaching, is about personal relationships and personal relationships are about trust.

Lack of trust is one of the main reasons players "fire" their coach. Players "fire" their coach in one of two ways:

1. By quitting and leaving
2. By not performing (quitting and staying)

If turnover, or low performance, is evident on your team, look for ways to establish more appropriate levels of trust.

Trust is built one encounter at a time and can be damaged or destroyed in one encounter. Listed below are several factors for establishing appropriate levels of trust:

♦ **Make and keep commitments.** Say what you will do and do what you say. When people know you are a person of integrity and they can count on you, their trust level goes up.

♦ **Take responsibility for your actions.** Admit mistakes and fix them.

♦ **Meet deadlines.** Give plenty of notice if you are going to miss one.

♦ **Be a good communicator.** Your ability to communicate can make or break relationships and your relationships can make or break your performance and results.

Relationships are built on trust and trust is developed over time and based on feedback.

♦ **Eliminate fear of the unknown in your relationships by being consistent.** Consistency enables predictability, predictability enables trust, and trust enables performance improvement. Consistency gives people comfort and inconsistency causes them discomfort. If you say one thing and do another, people will feel unsettled.

♦ **Avoid misunderstandings.** Fix them quickly if they do occur.

♦ **Do not have hidden agendas.** Most people can see right through them.

♦ **Minimize confusion.** Confusion causes uncertainty, uncertainty causes confusion, and confusion contributes to a reduction in trust.

♦ **Inspect what you expect.** People respect you more when you inspect what you expect.

Mutual respect and trust go hand in hand. When team members do not trust and respect each other, they are unwilling and unable to have a meaningful dialogue, which limits their ability to handle conflict constructively. The fear of letting down respected teammates can be a great motivator for people to improve their performance. In an atmosphere of mutual trust, teams can make timely decisions and move forward with complete buy-in from every team member – even those who spoke against the decision during the dialogue.

When there is a high level of trust and mutual respect on a

team, it is much easier and safer to speak with candor. Others are more likely to believe your message when they trust you and they are confident you have their best interest in mind.

Trust is the key to getting team members to maximize their energy. When there is tension in a relationship because of lack of trust, most, if not all, of a person's energy is spent on reducing the tension. When there is a relationship of mutual trust, tension is at a minimum and all energy can be used to complete tasks and accomplish goals.

Taking the time to establish and maintain trust in all your relationships will pay big dividends in every area of your life.

....

Action I will take to increase the trust levels in my relationships:

11

TEAM EFFECTIVENESS TIPS

- Identify what is needed to accomplish your goals and express them in terms of the daily activities necessary for achieving them.

- Identify individual and team priorities, put them in writing, and coach from them.

- Define what scoring and winning is for your team. When a team works together to accomplish a common goal, synergy is created and a winning tradition is more likely to take place.

- Make certain the best individual is in each position. Sometimes, the right people are on the team, but not necessarily in the right positions.

- Improve communication by keeping the appropriate people informed. Give early warning if a deadline is going to be missed or if a problem is occurring.

- Be on time.

- Be willing to be cross-trained and learn new jobs.

- Recognize opportunities where you can help, even if it is not in your job description.

- Look beyond your job and see the big picture.

- Offer input and ideas for improving processes and systems.

- Avoid unnecessary interruptions by making lists of what you need to discuss.

- Be willing to ask for and offer help.

- Have a positive attitude toward customers and team members.

◆ Clearly defined goals and expectations are essential for effective teamwork and optimum results. Specific goals and expectations deliver specific results. Unclear, vague goals and expectations typically produce no results. In order to assure acceptance of responsibility and consistency, people must understand what is expected of them.

◆ Stop listening to gossip, rumors, and complaints that you cannot do anything about. A commitment to stop listening to things you cannot do anything about can have several positive effects:

  » People learn to stop "dumping" on you.

  » Time is not wasted worrying about things you have no control over.

  » Reputations are not destroyed.

When someone wants to engage in gossip, rumors, or complaints with you, suggest that they talk with someone who can do something about their concerns. By encouraging co-workers to be proactive about their concerns, you can reduce incidences of gossip, rumors, or complaints. As a result, you and your team members can enjoy greater productivity and a more positive work environment.

....

Action I will take to improve the effectiveness of our team:

12

TIPS FOR IMPROVING TEAM PRODUCTIVITY

1. Show appreciation for team members' work and their contributions to the accomplishment of your team's goals.

2. Provide opportunities for training and learning.

3. Match talents to roles as best you can.

4. Treat each team member as an individual; get to know what is important to each team member; keep in mind that it is hard to motivate a stranger.

5. Create a balance between striving for productivity improvements and developing team members.

6. Expect, recognize, and reward excellence and outstanding performance.

7. Confront inappropriate behavior without being confrontational.

8. Insist that decisions be made at the lowest possible level.

9. Formulate development plans for each team member; get their concurrence.

10. Treat team members with dignity and respect; encourage them; give them hope.

11. Take pride in your team members' productivity, and let them know it.

12. Create a climate of mutual trust among team members;

avoid manipulation.

13. Ask good questions and be a good listener; listen for meaning as well as words; also, listen for what isn't said.

14. Use the magic question, "What do you think?" to build the confidence of team members and empower them to solve problems and make good decisions.

```
WHAT DO YOU THINK?
```

••

The tips I will work on first include:

The actions I will take to implement these tips include:

13
IMPROVING MORALE ON YOUR TEAM

Good team morale is one of the most important outcomes of a successful coach. Successful coaches take great pride in high morale and team spirit. They know when people work together as a team, their capacity for improving performance and results are dramatically expanded. They also know that high morale starts with them. Business leaders are, in essence, coaches. Their job is to bring out the best in their employees and help their team win. Getting and keeping the morale at a high level is one of the most important jobs of an effective leader.

Here are eight things you and your coaches can do to improve morale, performance, and results in your organization:

1. **Know Your People.** It is difficult to motivate a stranger. The more you know about your people, the more effective you will be at improving morale. What are their unique abilities; likes and dislikes; wants and needs? Do you know their goals? If not, why not? Do you know about their families? What are their hobbies and interests? What's most important to them?

2. **Keep People Informed.** Being in on things is one of the most powerful motivators for most people. When management fails to provide information the dangerous rumor-mill kicks in.

3. **Make People Feel Important.** Let them know, in as many ways as possible, that their contributions are important to the success of the organization.

4. **Listen to People.** One of the easiest ways to make

people feel important and increase their contribution is to listen to them.

5. **Keep Score.** Uncertainty contributes to low morale. If players don't know how to win on a daily basis, they will think there is no way to win, which leads to why try, which leads to low morale.

6. **Always Celebrate Improvement.** Look for improvement, no matter how small, and reinforce it with positive recognition. What gets rewarded gets done.

7. **Conduct Regular Coaching Sessions.** Focus on desired results and the behaviors needed to produce those results. Each coaching session needs to include the status of current results, the desired results, behaviors needed, by coach and player, to reach the results, and action steps that will be taken between coaching sessions.

8. **Give Appropriate Feedback.** Give frequent feedback. The severest form of criticism is not to find fault but to ignore someone. Give positive feedback. Positive feedback encourages and builds up. Negative feedback destroys initiative and morale. Give specific feedback that reinforces the behavior you want repeated for success.

Look for the following warning signs of a need to improve morale in your organization:

♦ In-fighting/friction/stress
♦ Turf protection
♦ Excessive meetings
♦ Low productivity/profitability

- Turnover/absenteeism
- Working at cross-purposes
- Majoring on minors
- Quality issues
- Safety issues
- Lack of new ideas/innovation
- Lack of teamwork
- Missed deadlines

•••

The morale on my team is:

Very Low   *Very High*

1   2   3   4   5   6   7   8   9   10

I chose this rating because:

Action I will take to maintain and/or improve morale:

14
MOTIVATING PEOPLE TO PRODUCE

Most people have an unlimited potential to produce great results in their chosen field. Their only limitations are usually ones they place on their own mind. People can change; they can be motivated to be more and do more. Unfortunately, most people will not change because we need, want, or even when we tell them to change. They will only change their behavior when they change their attitude. If you want to change what people are doing, you have to change what they are thinking. To change what they are thinking, you have to change what you are saying and, perhaps, how you are saying it.

Motivating people to produce must be affected through attitude change if it is to be permanent. The commonly used methods of fear and incentives have been proven to be temporary.

Fear is based on threat or punishment. Sooner or later, people become totally subjected to fear and won't do anything without first being told. Or, they become immune to fear and only do enough to get by. Either way, people will not give you their best effort, use their full potential, or get the results you want when fear is predominant in the culture.

Incentives are external rewards. They are designed to "lure" people to do something that they should have done in the first place. Incentives can work up to a point, but they will not provide long-lasting motivation. You will find that you have to give more and more for less and less.

Basically, an attitude is the way people think about

themselves and their circumstances. When, you, as a leader or coach, help people change the way they think, you help them change their attitude, which affects their behavior and influences their results. Here are some things you can do to motivate people to produce:

1. **Help them crystallize their goals.** When people have a clear picture of exactly what they want, they do not need to be forced or rewarded externally to accomplish the goal.

2. **Focus on their strengths.** People will grow quicker and accomplish more when they concentrate on their strengths and compensate for their weaknesses rather than being reminded of their weaknesses.

3. **Use positive reinforcement.** Point out people's accomplishments and progress. Catch them doing things right. When you see it, say it. What gets noticed and reinforced gets repeated. Make sure you recognize what you want repeated, not what you don't.

4. **Expect their best performance.** People tend to live up or down to a leader's expectations. Expect little and you will receive little. Expect great performance and results and you are more likely to get them.

When you help people develop the attitudes necessary for peak performance and success, they will develop the confidence to reach for higher and more meaningful goals and will be more valuable to you and your organization. They will discover solutions for themselves and not depend on outside circumstances. They will understand that in order to change their circumstances, they must first change themselves.

15
"IF IT'S TO BE, IT'S UP TO ME"

Here are 12 steps for achieving more of what you want out of your career and life:

1. **Have a written and specific goals program - both personal and business.** When you know where you stand, where you want to go, and how you're going to get there, you will have more confidence and be more motivated to achieve. It's important that your goals are in writing because writing crystallizes thought and crystallized thought motivates action.

2. **Exhibit initiative.** Someone once said, "Well-started is half-done." Another common saying is, "He who hesitates is lost." Getting started is critical to your success.

3. **Demonstrate self-reliance.** Once you get started, keep going. Two of my favorite sayings that support this point are: "Winners never quit and quitters never win." and "It is always too soon to quit."

4. **Accept personal responsibility.** This is the heart of the "if it is to be, it is up to me" concept. There will always be obstacles to any worthwhile goal. The way you respond to these obstacles and the choices you make as a result of them will determine the magnitude of your success. Remember, it's not your situation that affects the outcome, it's your reaction to the situation.

5. **Prepare yourself.** A commitment to continuous growth is essential in the pursuit and achievement of worthwhile goals. You'll be no better off tomorrow than you are today except for the books you read, the

messages you listen to and the people you associate with. If you want to have more, you need to be more.

6. **Believe in yourself.** Make a list of your personal strengths and past accomplishments. Review your list and add to it on a regular basis. By focusing on your strengths instead of your weaknesses and on your accomplishments instead of your problems, you will bolster your belief in yourself. This bolstered belief will help you break through obstacles, roadblocks and hindering circumstances.

7. **Visualize your success.** "Objects in mirror are closer than they appear" is etched in every automobile's passenger-side mirror. Put symbols of your future accomplishments on your bathroom mirror. You will soon discover that the accomplishment of these goals is closer than you thought.

8. **Establish and maintain relationships.** We usually need other people to help us reach our goals whether it's in a support role or direct assistance. Establishing, maintaining, and nurturing relationships will pay big dividends.

9. **Take appropriate risks.** Achieving worthwhile goals requires extra effort, persistence, determination, an "I will not be denied" attitude, and a "whatever it takes" attitude.

10. **Expand your resources.** Unless your goal is highly personal, you can usually get other people to help you achieve it. You can enlist family members, friends, or business associates.

11. **Be "on fire" about your goals.** When you're excited about your goals and enthusiastic about the outcome,

you'll draw on inner resources that will help your goals become reality.

12. **Commit to greatness.** To achieve great goals, you need to be the best you that you're capable of becoming. You need to make your life extraordinary. You need to develop and use more of your talents and abilities.

16
THE POWER OF DECISION-MAKING

People who fail to succeed, without exception, have the habit of reaching decisions very slowly and of changing their decisions very slowly.

Some never decide at all, but live in the misery of their indecisiveness. Indecision is a habit acquired in youth, and it unfortunately follows many people to the grave. By nature and habit, these people are usually easily influenced by the opinions and advice of others. They tend to accept this outside advice because subconsciously they want someone to share the blame should a failure result or the decision cause them problems.

Remember this: opinions are the world's cheapest commodity. If you are easily influenced by the opinions of others, you will never have an honest desire of your own.

Procrastination is the opposite of decision. It is a deadly enemy that each of us must conquer if we want to be in control of our own lives. My favorite definition of procrastination is "suicide on the installment plan."

Doubt is another obstacle that keeps people from making good decisions. Doubt is usually the result of a lack of self-knowledge and self-confidence. When people know who they are, where they stand, and where they are going, self-confidence is assured and good decisions will follow. William Shakespeare had this to say about doubt: "Our doubts are traitors and make us lose the good we oft might win, by fearing to attempt."

The world will stand aside for a person who can make a decision and take action. Once someone breaks through a barrier, everyone else believes that it can be done.

Each of us has the potential for achieving greater success. Rid your mind of limitations, and let the larger YOU come through. You will never know what you can do until you have tried. Nothing is too good to be true.

Other people will never be as excited about your goals, dreams and ambitions as you are. Even your loved ones and close personal friends will think of dozens of reasons why you shouldn't or couldn't do something. Be very selective when you seek advice about what you should or should not do.

In his book, *Your Greatest Power*, J. Martin Kohe wrote that our greatest power is the power of CHOICE. We can choose to be happy or sad, positive or negative, caring or mean, enthusiastic or dull. Here are a few things you can do to help you know you are making good decisions:

- **Have written and specific goals.** When you know where you stand, where you are going and how you are going to get there, you will usually make the right decision.

- **Use clear, objective thinking.** Ask yourself penetrating questions about what you want, why you want it, what it will look like etc. When you answer these questions honestly, the right decision will become apparent.

- **Tune in to your "feeling" on the matter.** When you have written and specific goals and have used clear, objective thinking, it is time to trust your instincts.

17
HAVING FUN HELPS YOU WIN

Twenty years ago I volunteered to coach my daughter's fourth grade basketball team. That experience was so much fun I volunteered the next five years as well. It was a tremendous bonding experience with my daughter and I learned a lot about leadership, communication, motivation, time management and many other things that have served me well in my business and personal life.

The first day of practice I told those young girls that we only had four rules on our team:

1. Have fun
2. Do your best
3. Learn & Improve
4. Win

They enthusiastically agreed that having fun was our most important goal. They also agreed that doing their best would give them a sense of pride, which is a form of having fun, and that learning and improving was also important for having fun. I concluded this first "pep" talk by saying that from my experience it was always a whole lot more fun to win than it was to lose.

Years later it occurred to me that these same principles applied to business. When a friend of mine was promoted to president of a large employee-owned company many of his speeches included how important it was to have fun at work. One employee gave him a bumper sticker that asked the question "ARE WE HAVING FUN YET?" My friend had that bumper sticker prominently displayed near the door to his office. Through employee-ownership his company has enjoyed a ten fold increase in revenue and has been very successful in many other ways also. This is a great example of having fun and winning in the process.

Having fun isn't about frivolous activity, it's about having a passion and enthusiasm about your work in the same way you do about your hobbies or recreational pursuits. Be enthusiastic about and have a passion for your work and it will be more fun. Instill the same kind of "having fun" mentality in your team members and you'll have even more fun.

Doing your best is more about excellence than perfection. When you do your best and you know it, energy is generated that allows you to do even more in the future. When you accept less than the best from yourself and those you lead, you and your team members miss out on this energy rush.

The legendary college basketball coach, John Wooden, said it best, "It's what we learn after we know it all that really matters." To be great at anything requires that you want to improve, set a goal to improve, get feedback on your performance, and practice purposely to improve. What do you want to improve about yourself and your leadership ability? What books are you reading? What CD's are you listening to? What seminars are you attending? What skills are you purposely practicing? What talents are you developing – in yourself and those you direct?

And, finally, have you defined "winning" for yourself and your team in specific terms that can be put on a scoreboard? Is there a tracking system in place that gives you feedback on your performance and that of your team? If not, do whatever it takes to define winning and start keeping score.

- ♦ ARE YOU HAVING FUN YET?

- ♦ ARE THE MEMBERS OF YOUR TEAM HAVING FUN YET?

When you encourage team members to do their best, help them learn and improve, and show them how to win individually and as a team, they will have more fun – and you will too.

18
DEVELOP AN "ABUNDANCE" MENTALITY

In any endeavor, our success is dependent on many factors. One factor that might be overlooked is having an abundance mentality. An "abundance mentality" is more than having a positive mental attitude, although a positive mental attitude is very important. When you have a positive mental attitude, you look at how things can be done rather than why they can't be done. You believe that "where there's a will, there's a way." You look at possibilities and opportunities rather than obstacles and problems. This mindset is important for success in any endeavor.

An abundance mentality will take you beyond a positive mental attitude. It will eliminate small thinking and offset negative energy. It can mean the difference between success and failure, excellence and mediocrity, and prosperity and despair. People with an abundance mentality believe the following:

- "The more I sell, the more there is to sell."
- "The more I give, the more there is to give."
- "The more I know, the more there is to know."
- "People are great. They will help me reach my goals."
- "If I need money, I'll find the money."
- "If I need people, I'll find the people."
- "If I need ideas, the ideas will come."

People with an abundance mentality believe there are enough resources available to accomplish their goals. They also believe that their success doesn't mean failure for others. On the contrary, the more successful they are, the more others are affected in a positive way. They can be happy when friends and associates prosper. They can enter every business transaction with a "win/win" attitude. They win when their clients win.

Here are some things that you can do to boost and enhance an abundance mentality:

♦ **Make a commitment to continuous growth.** Set up a reading, listening, watching and learning schedule. Participate in seminars and corporate development programs.

♦ **Help others grow.** A wise philosopher once said, "When you help another person get to the top of a mountain, you will arrive there also." Teach the people on your team what you know. If you have a talent for coaching or teaching children, volunteer. Seeing people grow as a result of your efforts will enhance your abundance mentality.

♦ **Have a written, specific goals program.** Review your goals daily, and update your action steps and accomplishments.

♦ **Utilize the synergy of a support group.** Join one or more organizations that have members who share your interest in personal and professional development and who support you in the process.

Abundance starts in your mind. The more you think abundantly, the more abundance you can enjoy. The more abundance you enjoy, the more success you will enjoy.

19
WHAT MAKES A LEADER DIFFERENT?

All of us know leaders who stand out in a crowd, who have risen to the top and who accomplish significantly more than their peers. Let's examine some of the characteristics that make these leaders different:

♦ **VISION -** Leaders have a clear picture of what they see their group becoming or doing in the future. There's a difference between eyesight and vision. Vision is the ability to get MEANING from eyesight. Effective leaders have vision.

♦ **GOAL-DIRECTED -** Leaders know where they stand, where they're going and how they're going to get there. They realize that no one ever accomplishes anything of consequence without a goal. Leaders also realize that in order to fulfill their vision, they need a series of goals that will help them do so. Effective leaders are goal-directed.

♦ **CLEAR PURPOSE -** Leaders know why they exist, what they believe and what their values are. Having a clear purpose gives them the energy and focus they need to accomplish their goals and fulfill their vision. Effective leaders have a clear purpose.

♦ **SELF-CONTROL/SELF-DISCIPLINE -** Leaders are many times required to do things that ordinary people don't like to do. The truth of the matter is, leaders probably don't like to do them either. The difference between a leader and an ordinary person is that a leader does whatever it takes to accomplish the goal, and many times this requires self-control and self-discipline. Effective leaders have self-control and self-discipline.

◆ **ABILITY TO COMMUNICATE** - To achieve their goals and fulfill their vision, leaders need to persuade others to take action on their ideas. This requires that they think clearly, speak clearly and listen carefully. Effective leaders have the ability to communicate.

◆ **ENERGY** - Leaders need the physical vitality and mental alertness that comes from a high level of energy. Hard work, clear thinking, commitment and persistence require a high level of energy. Leaders boost their energy through proper diet, nutrition, exercise, positive thinking, rest, relaxation and an outside hobby or interest. Effective leaders have a high level of energy.

◆ **PERSISTENCE** - There are only two reasons why most projects fail: not starting and not finishing. Leaders finish what they start because they remember their vision, focus on their goals and visualize their goals as already accomplished. They have the staying power and persistence to follow through on their goals regardless of circumstances or what other people say, think, or do. Effective leaders have persistence.

◆ **POSITIVE ATTITUDE** - Leaders look at how things can be done, not why they can't be done. They look for ways over, around, or through obstacles. They have an "I will not be denied" attitude. To paraphrase W. Clement Stone, "There is little difference between ordinary people and leaders. The little difference is attitude. The big difference is whether the attitude is positive or negative." Effective leaders have a positive attitude.

To be a more effective leader, clarify your vision and purpose. Develop a written and specific goals program. Develop your self-control, self-discipline and ability to communicate. Maintain a high energy level by taking care of your mind and body. Persist in all you do, and approach every challenge and opportunity with a positive attitude. Do these things and you'll not only be different, but you'll also MAKE A DIFFERENCE.

••

Actions I will take to make a difference:

20
HUMAN ASSETS OF SUCCESSFUL MANAGERS

- Steps up and can make tough decisions; pulls the trigger.

- Good communicator, good listener, and likes the interaction with people.

- Offers innovative ideas and effective solutions to critical operational problems.

- Understands his/her personal weaknesses and builds a complimentary team to fulfill the tasks at hand, covering individual weaknesses.

- Knows how to build trust among the people around him/her; very credible.

- "Vision" seems to be his/her forte; their thought process just seems right for the organization and its future success.

- Has good timing. Seems to know what is right for the organization at the right time; asks penetrating questions and exercises good judgment.

- Has the "Arnold Palmer" factor; the magnetism. Exercises "people skills;" people just want to be around this person as a mentor and as a leader.

- Has a deep understanding of how the company makes money and appreciates the contribution of each individual department to that end.

- Demonstrates "marketing skills" and helps create a

"customer focus" in the organization.

- ◆ "High energy" person who is results oriented. And, knows how "to keep many balls in the air" but has an excellent sense of priority.

- ◆ Is open to new ideas and is willing to change his/her point of view.

- ◆ Smart person in terms of I.Q. but, more so, has "street smarts;" intuitively perceives patterns of external change and can adapt "vision" to these changes.

- ◆ Has "quick study" characteristics. Is always curious, an observer, who acts rather than reacts.

- ◆ Has a track record of personal success. Strong record of extra-curricular activities in college and in career, helping to make her/him a well-rounded individual.

- ◆ Understands the concept of "value creation" and the relationship to the top line and bottom line.

- ◆ Has high moral/ethical standards and brings a sense of integrity to the company.

- ◆ Has a track record of removing "barriers to change" and is not content with the "status quo." In most cases believes that "sacred cows make the best hamburger."

- ◆ Loves interaction with "stakeholders." Loves the job, the people, and loves spreading the word.

- ◆ Has a "life," not just the work place. Is well read, knows how to get educated well beyond formal education. Is up on current events. Has a handle on what's happening out there.

♦   Knows how to balance work life and personal life.

*Excerpted with permission from *Return of the Body Snatchers*
by Cary Blair & Ron Watt

....

Actions I will take to be a more successful manager:

21

BEWARE OF OVER-MEASUREMENT

"When performance is measured, performance improves. When performance is measured and reported back, the rate of improvement accelerates."

–Thomas Monson

Extensive research supports the concept that feedback improves performance. But recently, we've observed that many organizations may be going overboard with the quantity, use, and management of information.

Just because we can measure something doesn't mean we should. A pretty graph or chart doesn't necessarily provide us the information we need to make decisions, plan for the future, or motivate individuals to take the proper action to improve results. Organizations fill their computers with measurements of all kinds. Companies seem to be obsessed with tracking, using excel spreadsheets, graphs, indexes, resolution times, throughput percentages, and on and on. Although feedback is critical to organizational performance, it can be useless unless it has a clear and specific purpose.

When was the last time you thought about those charts, graphs and reports and asked yourself if they really had any value?

♦ Is the report providing you with the information you need to improve results?

♦ Is it providing your people with critical feedback so they can make adjustments?

♦ If not, why are you using that report?

Next time you review your reports, consider the following to see if they are useful to you:

1. **Is the feedback specific?** Vague feedback provides information that is difficult to use to take action. Target something that individuals can understand.

2. **Is the feedback timely?** When feedback is given too infrequently, the gap between the desired objective and the current situation can be a major problem. Too frequent and employees spend more time on the measurement than the work being measured. The right amount of feedback provides valuable information in time to allow for adjustments.

3. **Do employees really use it?** Have you asked your employees if they understand the information they're reviewing? Or are they gathering it only to produce reports requested by management? Question the underlying assumption, "We've always done it that way."

4. **Does it help employees understand and eventually modify their performance on a daily, weekly, or monthly basis?** Measurement should motivate individuals to do better in the area that's being measured. Make sure that what you are measuring supports the real goals of the organization.

Any athlete will tell you that feedback is essential to improving performance. Any dietician can tell you that it can be either a motivator or the opposite. Too much feedback increases confusion and frustration and has little value. Think of the hours to be saved by simplifying or even eliminating unnecessary feedback and measurement. Simplifying these functions can save time in gathering data and producing reports, but more importantly it should increase efficiency by generating the important results you're really looking for.

....

Improvements in the way I will give feedback include:

22
GETTING PEOPLE TO FOLLOW YOUR LEAD

Members of your team will not necessarily follow your lead just because you've been given the title manager or supervisor. Unless you earn their respect, you might get insincere agreement, passive resistance, or a minimum effort. With their respect, you can have motivated team members who go the extra mile, initiate work, follow through, and contribute creative ideas for improvement.

Listed below are actions you can take to earn the respect of your team members, co-workers, and bosses:

- **Be Credible** – say what you will do and do what you say.

- **Be Trustworthy** – tell the truth, even if it is painful (to you).

- **Be Respectful** – treat others the way you would like to be treated; or, better yet, treat others the way they want to be treated.

- **Be Consistent** – most people have a strong fear of the unknown. When team members aren't sure how you will respond in a given situation, it causes a degree of fear and they do not do their best work in an aura of fear. Conversely, when you are consistent and team members can predict your reaction, they will feel safe and be more likely to perform at an optimum level.

- **Be Supportive** – you are a resource for your team members. Your job is to help them perform at a high level and be productive so they will be successful for the organization. Being supportive by providing resources and removing obstacles is a big part of your responsibility.

- ♦ **Be Appreciative** – your team members trade their performance for your appreciation, approval, and applause. It doesn't take much time or effort to say "thank you" or to comment on someone's work. This attentiveness will pay big dividends in team member loyalty, motivation, and performance.

- ♦ **Be Humble** – encourage team members to feel that you can identify with them by using some form of self-disclosure. For example, "I felt the same way when that happened to me;" or "A similar thing happened to me;" or "I ran into a similar problem on one of my projects."

Managers tend to overestimate the control they have by position authority and underestimate the influence they have by treating people with dignity and respect, being supportive, showing appreciation, and by being credible, trustworthy, consistent, and humble.

Rate yourself in the areas listed above and set goals to improve in those areas that you wish you could have rated higher. Then, enjoy the benefits of having people follow your lead because they want to, not because they think they have to.

•••

Improvements I will make to be a better leader include:

23
WHO HAS THE POWER?

A common misconception is that authority is bestowed. To the contrary, authority must be earned. Titles are bestowed and it is usually assumed that control and power come with the title. As a result, most managers overestimate the amount of control or power they have and tend to underestimate how much they can influence outcomes.

Authority is the right to decide no and the right to say yes. If someone has the right to decide either yes or no, but not both, they do not have authority. They have the illusion of authority. Empowering someone in an organization to decide no, but not yes, can limit performance and productivity. Authority (the ability to say yes or no) can and must be delegated. In addition, the limits of authority must be clearly defined. Freedom is greatest when boundaries are clearly defined. When people know exactly what their authority entails, they will be more confident to make correct decisions.

Power is the capacity to grant and withhold cooperation. You are a manager because there is a job to get done that you cannot do alone. If you cannot do it alone, you will need the cooperation of others. Therefore, anyone whose cooperation is needed has power. If a manager had both authority and power, everyone would cooperate automatically to get the job done.

A management problem arises when those with power (employees) refuse to cooperate. This lack of cooperation can be manifested in not getting work done at all or correctly, through slowness and delays, and poor quality. Attempts to gain cooperation with authority usually result in bribery or intimidation. If either of these methods worked consistently, most managers would not be needed.

The best way to deal with power (cooperation) is influence. Influence is the ability to get people to cooperate because it is in their best interest to do so. In order to influence people, you need to know what motivates them. To know what motivates them, you need to get to know them as a person because it's hard to motivate a stranger.

To get to know the people on your team, observe them, talk with them, listen to them and find out:

- What they are interested in
- What's important to them
- What they are proud of/what gives them a sense of pride
- What they do for pleasure
- What benefits they want to gain
- What pain they want to avoid
- What motivates them (it's OK to ask them)
- What type of feedback or recognition they prefer

Taking the time to get to know your team members will pay big dividends through better cooperation, improved motivation and morale, and improved performance and results.

....

Actions I will take to get to know my people better include:

24

TIPS FOR USING AUTHORITY

The proper use of authority will help you influence the people whose cooperation is needed to accomplish the tasks to be completed for the achievement of your organizational goals. The following ten points will help you use authority properly:

1. **Develop trust.** It's not automatically given; it must be earned. Be a person of integrity. Say what you are going to do and do what you say. Treat people fairly and with dignity and respect.

2. **Openly communicate more than you have to or need to.** Make it your top priority. Communication, like nature, abhors a vacuum. In the absence of communication, people will create their own messages, typically in the form of rumor, innuendo, and gossip.

3. **Be as specific as possible in the words and phrases you use.** Most conflicts and controversies are caused by people not understanding one another. When you use specific, easy to understand words and phrases, you increase the likelihood of being understood.

4. **Supply whatever background information and reasons people need to understand changes.** General George S. Patton is quoted as saying, "Never tell people how to do things. Tell them what to do, and why, and they will surprise you with their ingenuity."

5. **Be absolutely honest with all employees.** If you lie, or sugar-coat the truth, your credibility will be destroyed.

6. **Actively share information.** One of the strongest motivators for people is to be "in on things." Hoarding information doesn't give you power, sharing it does.

7. **Talk to an employee as one adult to another.** Even if employees act like children, resist the temptation to treat them like children. People will live up or down to your expectations. When you treat people like adults, they are more likely to act in a mature way. When you are condescending toward people or treat them with disdain, they will feel it and resent you for it.

8. **Always solicit employee ideas, suggestions, and reactions.** Everybody wants to feel important and can feel important when somebody understands and believes in them. It doesn't take much effort to make people feel important. Little things, done deliberately, at the right time, can make a big difference. Soliciting ideas, suggestions, and reactions will not only make people feel important, you might be surprised at what you learn.

9. **Follow through, always - no exceptions.** As a manager or supervisor, you are on stage all the time. If you don't follow through, or if you drop the ball, you can expect your employees to do the same thing.

10. **Recognize the job of a manager is to remove roadblocks, irritants, and frustrations - not put them there.** When you remove roadblocks, irritants, and frustrations, you help your employees become successful and you will be successful also.

....

Ways that I will improve how I use authority include:

25
"NO NEWS" IS NOT GOOD NEWS

"No news is good news" is a destructive philosophy when it comes to bringing out the best in people. Average leaders will spend equal time with everyone or, worse yet, spend most of their time with problem people they call "high maintenance." Great leaders spend more time with their top producers.

An important part of a leader's job is to bring out the best in each team member in order to achieve the goals of the organization. The behaviors the leader reinforces will determine the productivity of the team.

When leaders spend more time with team members who display poor behavior and produce poor results, they are taking time away from top producers who display good behavior and good results. Common thinking is "if it isn't broke, don't fix it," and some leaders apply this flawed thinking to top producers who "aren't broke."

A basic principle of human behavior is "what gets rewarded gets repeated." When you reward poor behavior by paying attention to it, you will get more poor behavior. Conversely, when you ignore good behavior, you will get less of it. Human beings need and respond to attention, especially from the important people in their lives.

When you ignore, or spend too little time with, top performers because you are spending too much time with poor performers, you will get the opposite of what you want – poor performance, low productivity, and poor results.

When you see a top performer's behavior change for the worse, it is likely that you have been paying attention to the wrong people. Great leaders spend time with top performers because this investment will produce the best results, it rewards the best behavior and best performers, and it is the right thing to do. Also, by helping the strong get stronger, you raise the bar and might inspire low performers to change their behavior.

Look at where you are spending your time. If you are spending too much time with strugglers, make a conscious effort to spend more time with your best performers and see how they respond. Remember, "no news" is destructive and doesn't bring out the best in people. Positive reinforcement is constructive and gets you more of the behaviors you want.

•••

Action I will take to spend appropriate time with top performers:

26
HOW TO ENERGIZE PEOPLE

Energy, not time, is the fundamental currency of high performance. Performance, health and happiness are grounded in the skillful management of energy. The number of hours in a day is fixed, but the quantity and quality of energy available to us is not. It is our most precious resource.

As a leader, you are the steward of your team members' energy. Here are 10 things you can do to keep energy at a high level on your team:

1. **Say what you will do and do what you say.** When people know you are a person of integrity and they can count on you, their trust level goes up and they can use their energy in productive pursuits.

2. **Help people remember their past successes.** People have a tendency to vividly remember their past mistakes and failures and forget or diminish their past successes. By helping them remember their past successes, you help them boost their energy.

3. **Help people set short-term goals and break more complex goals into "bite-sized," chunks.** When people enjoy frequent successes, they become energized. The saying that "success breeds success" is absolutely true. Small successes lead to big successes.

4. **Look for opportunities to recognize and praise people.** Praise is a great elixir. It builds self-esteem, bolsters self-image, and creates an adrenalin rush that generates an abundance of energy. Praise is the catalyst for energy.

5. **Help people focus on the next step.** When people realize the power of progressive realization and develop an "I can do that (next step)" attitude, improved performance and success are inevitable which, in turn, helps create more energy.

6. **Help people identify their passion.** Passion creates energy. When people know what their passion is and take steps to pursue and fulfill it, they are going to be energized.

7. **Inspect what you expect.** People respect you more when you inspect what you expect. This helps people become more accountable, and being accountable produces energy.

8. **Keep score.** Keeping score helps people know whether they are winning or losing and stamps out uncertainty. Certainty creates energy. Uncertainty drains energy. As a leader, one of your most important jobs is to help stamp out uncertainty.

9. **Encourage people.** When people feel encouraged, they can overcome incredible adversity. Overcoming adversity builds self-esteem and generates more energy.

10. **Help people bring out their enthusiasm.** Enthusiasm gives people energy. It creates a positive aura and helps people relax and feel confident.

Being fully engaged in work you enjoy generates energy. A high energy level will help you feel invigorated, confident, challenged, joyful, and connected. All of these characteristics will help you be the "generator" for the members of your team.

Excerpted from *The Power of Full Engagement* by Jim Loehr, Ed.D., Chairman & CEO, Human Performance Institute and Tony Schwartz.

••

Steps I will take to energize people:

27
FOCUS ON STRENGTHS

From early childhood, we are conditioned to "fix" our weaknesses. When adults are asked to list their strengths, most of the time it is a struggle for them to list more than a few. When those same adults are asked to list their weaknesses, a much longer list is usually forthcoming.

Most adults have been exposed to numerous people in positions of authority who were determined to help them fix what was wrong with them. In other words, fix their weaknesses. Most managers spend an inordinate amount of time working with weak performers and focusing on mistakes. It is a myth to think that fixing weaknesses makes everything better. The best way to drive excellence is to focus on strengths and manage weaknesses.

Instead of focusing on weaknesses, determine the strengths of your team members and determine ways for them to spend more time in these areas and less time in their areas of weakness. Look for ways to offset weaknesses in one team member with the strengths of another. People are energized when they are working in their areas of strength. And, they are more motivated about their work. In the process their self-esteem is enhanced.

You can start an epidemic of positive energy on your team by making a conscious effort to seek out and acknowledge the strengths of your team members. Start by observing working behaviors in broad categories and then get more specific. Make a list for yourself and each team member. Look for how active each of you is or how much energy each of you has. Then, determine who has strengths in the following areas:

- Attention to detail
- Friendliness
- Creativity
- Follow-through
- Helpfulness
- Customer-oriented
- Community-minded
- Dedicated
- Enthusiasm
- Experience
- Maturity
- Organization
- Patience
- Punctual
- Reliable
- Sensitive
- Self-starting
- Stable
- Thoughtful
- Tolerant
- Trustworthy
- Versatile
- [If these descriptions don't work for you, create your own list.]

Create situations where you can spend a high percentage of your time in your areas of strength. Then, give your team regular feedback to reinforce the behaviors you want repeated. Doing this on a regular basis will produce an accumulative effect that will have a major impact on your performance, productivity, and results.

ACTION STEPS:

- ♦ Have high expectations for yourself and your team members.

- ♦ Find out what you and team members do well and do more of it.

- ♦ Find out what you and team members do not do well and stop doing it.

- ♦ Manage your weaknesses and help your team members manage theirs.

....

Expectations for myself and my team:

What I and team members do well:

What I and team members will stop doing:

Weaknesses I will manage better:

28
THE ROLE OF SELF-IMAGE
IN SUCCESS

Dr. Maxwell Maltz, a plastic surgeon, perpetuated a concept called "self-image psychology" in his best selling book, *Psycho-Cybernetics*. He discovered that many patients who had cosmetic or corrective plastic surgery continued to see themselves as ugly or disfigured. When scientists studied this phenomenon, they concluded that people have a conscious mind and subconscious mind. The conscious mind is where you do your thinking and it is working while you are awake. Most people only use their conscious mind about 10 percent of their waking hours.

Your subconscious mind works 24/7. It is made up of your memory bank and self-image. It records everything you have ever heard, read, or said. Unlike the conscious mind, your subconscious mind cannot tell the difference between fact and fantasy. It believes everything it hears and stores it in your memory bank and/or self-image. The reason you only use your conscious mind 10 percent of the time is that once your subconscious mind turns something into a habit, you do not have to think about doing something – it happens automatically and instinctively. This saves you time, but it also causes a problem when you try to change a habit.

> **A SELF-IMAGE ONCE STRETCHED WILL NOT RETURN TO ITS FORMER SHAPE.**

You think from your conscious mind. Your conscious mind explores your subconscious database to find the data that supports your thoughts or desired actions. If it is something you have done numerous times and turned into a habit, it will be in your memory bank and you will perform the action the same way you have on numerous occasions. If it is a new thought or desired action, the self-image portion of your subconscious mind comes into play. You will act based on what is in your self-image and get results accordingly. Your success, especially in new adventures, will be greatly determined by your self-image. It is a servo-mechanism that does whatever you tell it to, to the best of its ability.

Your self-image is developed by your thoughts; the books you read; what you listen to; the input you receive from friends, business associates, and family members; and your past experiences. Each positive experience puts a growth bump on your self-image. Each negative experience nicks or takes a chunk out of your self-image. That is why it is so important to focus on your strengths, have written and specific goals, and be mindful of your past accomplishments and victories. It is also important to feed your sub-conscious mind with positive input from the books you read, recordings you listen to, and the people you associate with. Your future success depends on it.

••

I will feed my mind with the following positive inputs (books, CDs, self-talk, etc.):

29

BRIDGING THE GAP BETWEEN PERFORMANCE AND POTENTIAL

There is always a gap between performance and potential. Sometimes it's a huge gap. Even in the most ordinary activity, no matter how good people are, they can always do better... thus a performance gap.

Interference of some type is usually the cause of the gap between performance and potential. To reduce this gap and increase performance, reduce the following forms of interference:

- Fear (of losing, of winning, of making a fool of oneself)
- Lack of self-confidence
- Trying too hard
- Trying for perfection
- Trying to impress
- Anger and frustration
- Boredom
- A too busy mind

One way to reduce interference is to focus attention. When attention is focused a person enters a mental state in which he/she can learn and improve. Anything you, as a coach, can do to help people focus their attention will pay big dividends in improved performance.

You can help a person perform at a higher level by working with the individual's capacity to learn. Your primary responsibility is to facilitate learning, not teach.

1. Start from the known (what the person knows and can prove about his/her current level of performance and/or ability) and move toward the unknown.

2. Have the person set a goal for improvement and establish a method for measuring progress and improvement.

Learning without achievement quickly exhausts one's energy. Achievement without learning soon becomes boring. Neither of these two outcomes will encourage further learning and improvement.

Create an environment where the person has a good opportunity to win, gets frequent feedback, and is aware of improvement and progress. Help the person celebrate small successes and improvements as well as the large ones.

Excerpted from *Effective Coaching* by Myles Downey, Founder, The School of Coaching

30

AVOIDING MISCOMMUNICATIONS

The biggest miscommunication is to assume communication has taken place. How many times have you been disappointed by someone you thought you communicated with, only to find out they were on a different page than you? This happens tens of thousands of times every day in business and personal relationships.

We can reduce miscommunications, missed expectations, frustration, confusion, disappointment, anger, and many other emotions by keeping the following things in mind when we are attempting to communicate:

1. **Know what your goal is.** What do you want the other person to know, think, or do?

2. **Choose your words carefully.** If possible, practice what you will say and/or write out what you want to say. Use words and language at the recipient's level.

3. **Use the proper tone and inflection.** Emphasizing different words in a sentence can dramatically change the way your message is perceived.

4. **Make certain your body language and facial expressions are congruent with your message.** People believe what they see over what they hear.

5. **Observe the body language and facial expressions of the other person.** If the other person's body language or facial expression isn't congruent with the message you are sending, stop and ask a question that will get you both on the same wave length.

6. **Pace yourself to the mental speed of your listener.** You can usually tell how fast a person thinks by how fast he or she talks. If you go too slow or too fast, the other person might get impatient, confused, or frustrated.

7. **Actively ask for feedback.** For example, "So we can be sure we are communicating effectively, would you tell me your understanding of what we just discussed?" If you are on the same page or wave length, move on. If not, clarify and discuss until you are. Avoid questions such as: "Do you understand?" or "Have I made myself clear?" Such closed-end questions can cause your listener to give you a tacit yes and, worse yet, feel that you think he or she is stupid, which can lead to shutting down communication.

8. **Control the environment as much as possible.** If there is a lot of noise, or other distractions, move to a quieter location with fewer distractions.

9. **Ask questions until you get to the heart of the matter or accomplish your goal.** Mix statements with your questions. People are good at answering questions. Also, a question can be perceived as threatening and can intimidate. Sometimes you can elicit information better with a statement than you can a question. A statement opens the door to the other person's reply. A statement does not require a reply, whereas a question does. For example, you can make a statement such as, "You are probably wondering about a number of things that are involved with these changes we are discussing". Even if the other person responds with a simple, "Yes", resist the temptation to speak. Use silence to give the other person the inclination to tell

you what he or she is really thinking. Knowing what the other person is thinking is the first step in avoiding miscommunications.

....

Action I will take to reduce miscommunications:

31
THE 10 COMMANDMENTS
OF COMMUNICATION

Whenever two or more people make contact, communication occurs. It can occur in person, by phone, through E-mail, in voice mail, during a video conference, at meetings or conferences, or at speeches or workshops.

Communication is the exchange of thoughts, messages, feelings, goals, or information. The key word is exchange. Unless an exchange takes place, communication has not occurred. The following 10 COMMANDMENTS OF COMMUNICATION are from *BUILDING A WINNING TEAM* by Harris "Hank" Plotkin, THE PLOTKIN GROUP:

1. Develop trust. It's not automatically given; it must be earned.

2. Openly communicate more than you have to or need to. Make it your top priority.

3. Be as specific as possible in the words and phrases you use.

4. Supply whatever background information and reasons people need to understand changes.

5. Be absolutely honest with all employees.

6. Actively share information and feelings.

7. Talk to an employee as one adult to another (the way you would like your boss to talk with you).

8. Always solicit employee ideas, suggestions, and

reactions.

9. Follow through, always --- no exceptions.

10. Recognize the job of a manager is to remove roadblocks, irritants, and   frustrations --- not put them there.

Abiding by the above 10 COMMANDMENTS OF COMMUNICATION will help you reduce miscommunications, missed expectations, frustrations, confusion, disappointments, anger, and will improve performance and results.

....

Action I will take to improve my communication results:

32

IMPROVING PERFORMANCE WITH CLEAR EXPECTATIONS

Giving specific, appropriate feedback is the quickest, cheapest, and most effective intervention for improving performance. Clarifying expectations is the first step in a coach's ability to give specific, appropriate feedback.

When people have to guess what they are supposed to do it creates tension and they won't do their best work. Avoid using general terms such as, "do your best," "try harder," "you need to be more thorough," etc. People have trouble knowing what "their best," "trying harder," or being "more thorough" looks like.

The enemy of accountability is ambiguity. Therefore, it is imperative that you publish written goals, expectations, and standards and manage from them:

1. Identify what the team needs to achieve. Most employees will make a great effort to hit the target when they know exactly what the target looks like.

2. Identify who needs to deliver what. Job expectations must be clear and easy to measure.

3. Identify how everyone must behave in order for the team to succeed.

Conduct regular, simple progress reviews to encourage open communication and get team members to take action that they otherwise might not take. Clear written expectations and open communication are the best investments you can make to get your team members thinking and acting in a manner conducive to achieving the desired results.

Reward team actions, progress, and results as much as possible. When you reward teamwork, cooperation, and personal accountability, you will get more of each.

Sometimes workers know they are doing things they should not be doing, but they don't realize it is a problem. To avoid this, ask employees:

♦ How do you know when you are doing a good or bad job?

♦ How do you measure the quality of your performance?

♦ How do you know when you do something wrong?

♦ Describe what good performance looks like.

♦ Describe what bad performance looks like.

When people clearly understand what is expected of them, it reduces the relationship tension and improves their ability to perform up to the coach's expectations.

33
TIPS FOR CONFRONTING INAPPROPRIATE BEHAVIOR

Many people think confrontation is negative. Childhood sayings run through their mind – for example, "If you cannot say anything nice about someone, don't say anything at all" or "Play nice." These thoughts can get in the way of appropriate confrontation.

If someone's behavior is inappropriate, you do him or her a disservice by not bringing it to his or her attention. Most, if not all, people want to know if their behavior is counter-productive for achieving the desired results and contributing to the team's success. Here are some guidelines for effective confrontation:

- ◆ Focus on specific issues or behaviors an employee can control. Avoid personal attacks.

- ◆ Deal with the facts. Avoid using rumors, innuendos, or sarcasm as a basis for confronting an employee.

- ◆ Avoid inflammatory words such as should, ought to, have to, always, never, etc. Instead, focus on desired goals, results, and appropriate behavior.

- ◆ Train yourself to listen for what's important or key to the issue, and "block" words like those listed in the previous bullet point.

- ◆ Be direct without being rude, obnoxious, or otherwise offensive.

- ◆ Treat the employee with dignity and respect and never show your anger. Remember, people will always remember how you made them feel long after the specific words are forgotten.

♦ Help the employee develop a plan of action for correcting an unproductive situation or inappropriate behavior.

♦ Approach the situation as soon as you have the facts and an opportunity to meet privately with the employee.

♦ End your session by stating your belief that the employee will do better in the future.

....

Action I will take to reduce, or eliminate, inappropriate behavior in our work group:

34

FREQUENT FEEDBACK PREVENTS PROBLEMS

Without feedback there is no improvement or progress. Most quality programs are based on getting feedback on how current processes work so they can be improved. Without the feedback, there would be no improvement. The same is true with human behavior; without appropriate feedback and positive reinforcement there will be no improvement in performance and results.

Effective coaches understand that giving appropriate feedback is the quickest, cheapest, and most effective method for improving performance and results.

Humans need feedback to validate their existence, enhance their self-esteem, and improve their self-image. One of the greatest forms of punishment is solitary confinement; little or no feedback. Our self-images are developed by feedback we get from experiences and/or other people. A Sunday school teacher told me I was a good reader when I was 11 years old. I believed her and have been an avid reader for the past 50 years, reading 50 plus books a year plus numerous magazines and articles. Did feedback affect my self-image and behavior? Absolutely! All of us can relate examples of how feedback has affected our behavior and performance.

As a coach, you have a unique opportunity to improve performance and shape results through the use of appropriate feedback. All feedback is important to performance improvement. Positive reinforcement is critical. People tend to act to gain a benefit or avoid a loss. People tend to gravitate toward pleasure and reward and avoid punishment and rejection. As a result, human behavior is driven by the principle that what gets rewarded, gets done.

If you want a sales person to make more calls, use positive reinforcement. If you want a sales person to open new accounts, use positive reinforcement. If you want a better safety record, or less waste or rework, or better accuracy, or on-time shipments, use positive reinforcement. Positive reinforcement is accomplished through feedback --- from a trusted, supportive coach.

The dilemma with feedback in business is that most people won't ask for feedback and most business coaches don't give enough of the right kind. Most people won't ask for feedback because they don't want to appear weak or perceived as "high maintenance" or they think if they have to ask for it, it isn't as valuable.

Business coaches don't give enough appropriate feedback for a myriad of reasons, including:

♦ They don't fully understand the value and importance.

♦ They don't know how.

♦ They don't think they have enough time; they are too busy "doing".

♦ They don't get enough from their coach.

♦ They have had poor role models in the past.

Since people are reluctant to ask for feedback, it is imperative that coaches make an extra effort to give appropriate feedback using positive reinforcement. Catch people doing things right. Focus on people's strengths and stop pointing out their weaknesses. Notice and comment on progress. When you see it, say it. When people see you are sincere about recognizing their contribution to the organization, you will be rewarded with improved performance and results, higher morale, better teamwork, and a more positive work environment.

I will do a better job of:

○ *Catching people doing things right*

○ *Focusing on people's strengths*

○ *Recognizing and commenting on progress*

35

FIXING PEOPLE PROBLEMS

One of a manager's most difficult jobs is dealing with people problems. Most managers have the tendency to ignore these problems and hope they will go away, or spend so much time dealing with them that they neglect those team members who are doing a good job. The ideas that follow will help you overcome these natural tendencies.

People problems fall into a lot of categories, e.g. tardiness, absenteeism, sloppiness, poor interpersonal relations, low performance, lack of cooperation, poor teamwork, insubordination, disruptive behavior, or breaking company rules, just to name a few.

Most minor issues or infractions can be corrected by simply addressing them in a gentle, straight-forward manner. This can often be done in a relaxed, casual setting. The better your relationship with the team member, the easier it will be to get an improvement in behavior.

However, if the problem persists and is having a negative impact on your team and productivity, you will need to let the employee know that some sort of resolution is imperative. This usually requires a more formal setting.

Virtually all employees want to be successful. They do not want to be viewed or considered as "high maintenance" or a problem. Sometimes the underlying problem is a feeling of being under-appreciated, or not being thought of as important to the team or organization.

Perhaps they have personal problems away from the job. Be

careful that you don't think of someone as "high maintenance" or a problem. It is important to focus on difficult or problem behaviors rather than difficult or problem people. This minor distinction can be a major factor in helping you maintain an objective, problem-solving attitude.

The costs of keeping poor performing employees are significant. The direct costs include increased labor, waste, rework, lost sales, poor customer relations, and damage to your reputation, to name a few. Team members who pick up the slack feel resentful and can lose their motivation. It will also be difficult for the manager to get other team members to perform at the desired level. The poorest performing employee usually sets the standards.

At the same time, the costs of replacing an employee can be substantial. The direct costs could include ad cost, placement fees, personnel testing, costs related to interviewing, and training costs. Other, harder to measure, costs could include: the cost of mistakes or errors, customer dissatisfaction or loss of confidence, and low team morale.

The Bottom Line – fixing an existing problem is usually less expensive than recruiting, hiring, and training a replacement employee.

••

I will fix the following people problem(s):

36

PRINCIPLES FOR DEALING WITH PEOPLE PROBLEMS

- Let people know the impact of their actions. Make sure the impact is relative to them, not you.

- Avoid E-mail when dealing with people problems. You will lose the effectiveness of tone, inflection, facial expression, and body language; plus, your message or intent might be misinterpreted without the advantage of a dialogue. Try to deal with the issue face to face. If that isn't practical, do it by phone.

- The severity of the problem might dictate the time needed, but in most cases be direct and keep it brief.

- Avoid showing anger. It is okay to show or express disappointment; or, to explain the gravity of the situation with intensity; but, getting angry will create unnecessary tension that could shut down communication and cause resistance to change.

- Get the team member to set a goal to correct the problem behavior. Set a follow-up date to review progress on the goal.

- Resist the temptation to raise your voice. Keep it at a normal level or slightly lower. This will help keep emotions in check and encourage the team member to listen.

- Describe your expectations for acceptable performance, behavior, or results in specific terms. Do not "sugar coat" or "beat around the bush." Get agreement or acknowledgement that the team member understands your expectations. Get the team member to tell you, in his or her own words, what your expectations are. A nod or passive approval is not enough when you are dealing with a serious problem.

- Get agreement that the current behavior is not meeting expectations and is unacceptable.

- Planning:
    - » Get the facts.
    - » Do not rely on rumor or innuendo.
    - » Know enough about the person to predict his or her responses.
    - » Write bullet points about what you will say in what order.
    - » Choose an appropriate location that is private.

- ASAP – when you become aware of a problem and have the facts, the best time to act is as soon as possible. Waiting will not make the situation better and it probably won't go away. If the temperature gauge in your car enters the danger zone and a hissing noise is coming from under the hood, delaying attention will not be very pleasant. Likewise, delaying attention to problem behavior can be damaging to you and your entire team.

- When challenged, the best strategy is to avoid over-reacting. Listen carefully and let the person vent. Venting to a good listener will usually make the other person more receptive to changing and taking corrective action.

- Avoid offering your personal opinion; keep the discussion business-based.

◆ When there are multiple issues, focus on one at a time to prevent overwhelming or confusing the team member.

◆ Document the conversation. This will make it easier to follow up and reduce the possibility that something was misconstrued.

◆ Be open to the possibility that this problem employee's behavior is a symptom of a larger problem within your team. Perhaps this person is in the wrong role; there are poor working conditions or a hostile working environment; or, there is a personality conflict with another team member.

....

Actions I will take to improve my ability to deal with people problems:

37
BUILDING A HIGH PERFORMANCE TEAM

Building a high performance team requires that you:
1. Know what you want your members to do.
2. Make sure they know what you want them to do.
3. Train them how to do it.
4. Motivate them to want to do it.

Signs of success:
At the start of a career, desire can make up for a lack of skills. People with initiative will watch how you do things that work well and will pick up good ideas on their own.

Stress that they can control what happens to them. Emphasize that they're responsible for their own actions and results and that you will support them in direct proportion to their commitment.

Work habits:
The major goal of developing good work habits is to stretch - to accomplish progressively larger goals. Train people to schedule high-payoff revenue-producing activities in prime time slots. Get them to do other activities in non-prime time.

How to grow people:
The goal of effective coaches is to "grow" people. People tend to concentrate more on their failures than on their successes and on their weaknesses more than their strengths. This induces self-doubt. When this occurs, don't commiserate with them; help them look for solutions. Worrying about negative

issues uses energy in a nonproductive way. People suffering from this negative syndrome may begin to procrastinate and become defensive and afraid that whatever they do will fail. They literally don't know what to do next and relive their past failures over and over. Help them focus on future success.

Look for positive things to praise people for, and remind them of the good days they've had. Point out progress no matter how slight it may be. Affirm their efforts to keep them from getting discouraged. "Inspect what you expect" to make sure the people you manage know what's expected of them in activity, performance and attitude. Being a good role model is one of the best ways you can help someone. Remember, the speed of the leader is generally the speed of the team.

How to motivate people:
If your team understands what you want them to do, they know how to do it and they have the competence to do it, there's only one reason why they aren't doing it: They don't want to. This is a motivation problem.

The first step in overcoming this motivation problem is to know your people. Keep a journal on what you learn about each of them: goals, strengths, weaknesses, progress, setbacks and daily activities. Regularly meet with your people one-on-one to discuss obstacles, how their week ahead is shaping up and how their short-range goals are coming along. When you know what your people want and why they want it, you will enhance your ability to build a high performance team.

38

INCREASING PERSONAL MOTIVATION

MOTIVATION can be defined as a desire held in expectation with the belief that it will be realized. In other words, motivation is a "motive for action," i.e. reason, purpose, or goal for doing something. Keep in mind that action, or behavior, includes both cause and effect. Motivation involves both the actions and the motive or cause behind the actions. Within reasonable limits, the needs, desires and drives of all people are fairly universal.

Our behavior is the action we take to satisfy desire, but different people take different paths to reach their goals. Two people may adopt identical behavior to reach opposite goals, or they may behave in diametrically opposite ways to achieve a similar goal.

Observe the behavior patterns of your employees as well as your own. Each person has his or her own set of conscious or unconscious goals, and these needs or goals motivate the chosen pattern of behavior. Therefore, all motivation is personal. To understand what it takes to motivate a person, we must know and understand the person as an individual. Each person has needs that must be satisfied.

Identify these personal needs and help each employee translate them into personal goals. Then, you can help the employee see how these personal goals will help the organization achieve its goals. Since motivation is personal, you motivate an entire organization one person at a time. There is no easier or simpler way. People are the medium through which all systems must pass.

Because employees reflect different heritages, environments and training, there is no single method or idea that will successfully motivate all of them all the time. Effective motivation can be accomplished only on a personal basis. Maintain an atmosphere that is conducive to personal motivation and individual growth by combining motivational management with each employee's desire for personal success.

People rarely strive to increase their personal motivation unless they are stimulated and led by enlightened and self-motivated leaders. As a leader, it is your responsibility to create a climate for growth and learn to deal with each employee's motivation on an individual basis.

To do this, you need to be observant, spend one-on-one time with each person, ask questions, listen and take a genuine interest in each person. Remember, all people have one thing in common – they are all different.

....

I will take the following action to be more observant, listen, and take a genuine interest in people:

IT'S HARD TO GET AWAY FROM A GOOD LISTENER

Listening involves more than your ears. It involves your eyes and any other senses you can put into play. When you see what a person pays attention to, you can tell what their intentions are. Listen to the words they use. Watch their facial expressions and body language. What is important to them? Are they using contradictory terms or phrases? Are they avoiding answering certain questions or skirting certain issues? Are they making eye contact? All of these are signals you can interpret to help you communicate. This is called active listening. Think of listening as a precious gift you are giving the other person. Even in the most difficult situations, people appreciate it when you listen.

Some of the Benefits of Active Listening Include:

- Prevent misunderstandings

- Improve insight into people's wants and needs

- Enhance relationships

- Increase opportunities to learn

- Reduce friction and resolve conflicts

- Enlist support and favorable responses

- Encourage a more honest and sincere exchange

People Fail to Hear Because They Are:

- Too busy preparing what they are going to say

- Letting their mind wander (We listen at least four times faster than we speak.)

- Lazy (It takes effort to listen effectively.)

- Faking attention

- Egotistical or mentally set (They lack interest in what other people are saying.)

- Impatient

To Encourage Others to Talk So We Can Listen:

- Will Rogers said, "Never miss a good opportunity to shut up." Most people have a favorite topic – themselves. Keep in mind that it is hard to get away from a good listener. People will think you are brilliant when you let them talk about themselves.

- Be sincerely interested in what other people are saying. People can sense insincerity and when they do they might get defensive, lose interest in the discussion, and/or otherwise shut down.

- Encourage people with supportive nods and phrases.

- Guide the conversation with questions. Remember, the question mark is mightier than the exclamation point.

- Avoid interrupting other people.

- Concentrate on what other people are trying to say – their words, ideas, and feelings related to the subject.

- Make eye contact.

- Stay in the moment. Compartmentalize any other issues that might distract you.

- Get rid of distractions. Put down papers or pencils, unless you are taking notes. Turn off your cell phone or put it on silent mode. Turn your computer monitor off and/or shutdown your computer or laptop.

- Ask for clarification if you do not understand a point or idea.

GIVE PEOPLE THE PRECIOUS GIFT OF LISTENING

....

Action I will take to be a more active listener:

40
HELP TEAM MEMBERS
DEVELOP THEIR TALENTS

Regardless of your product or service, you are in the people development business. Acquiring and keeping good people is one of your most important jobs. The more your team members grow and develop their talents and abilities, the more they will be able to accomplish. See your team members as they can become and encourage them to become what you see. People tend to become what the most important people in their lives think they will become; and, you are one of the most important people in the lives of your team members.

A great manager has the knack for making team members think they can become more than they are now. A great manager is one who brings out the best in his or her team members. Listed below are some ways you can help team members grow and bring out the best in them.

- ♦ **Encourage Personal Growth -** Give them opportunities to try new things and acquire new skills. Growth is motivating. Stagnation is boring and will sap a person's energy. Provide opportunities for learning. Give team members personal development books, tapes, and CDs. Conduct book studies. Send team members to seminars and other training opportunities

- ♦ **Be a Good Role Model -** When you are a student of continuous learning and personal growth, it will be easier to encourage your team members to embrace personal development and growth.

- ♦ **Encourage Personal Goal Setting -** When team

members accomplish personal goals, they have more confidence in themselves, their self-esteem expands, and they become more valuable employees. The personal goal doesn't need to have anything to do with work. When someone quits smoking, loses weight, starts a workout program, improves their golf game, spends more quality time with loved ones, or any other goal that is important to them, they will feel better about themselves and that will show up in their work.

♦ **Help Team Members Identify Their Strengths** - Their talents and abilities – and help them spend more time using these strengths, talents, and abilities. Developing strengths is more motivational, takes less effort, and gives a greater return on investment than trying to fix weaknesses. If team members have been toiling in areas where they are weak, and you reassign them to work in areas where they can use their strengths, you'll see a dramatic increase in natural motivation.

♦ **Look For Opportunities to Build Up Team Members** - Give them credit for their suggestions; seek their opinions; recognize or point out their progress or improvement.

♦ **Set Goals for Growth** - Make a list of your team members and identify what each of them can do to grow to the next level. Discuss what you have written with each team member, get their buy-in that they would like to accomplish the goal, and help them develop a written plan of action to achieve the goal. If, when you make your list, you discover some personal development goals common among team members, consider some group training that will address the goal area.

- **Set Up a Personal Development Library** - This can be a room, an area of a room, a book shelf, cabinet, or any other designated area that team members have access to. You can have a formal check-out system or use an honor system. The important thing is to make it as easy as possible for team members to have access to material that will help them grow, develop, and use more of their potential.

- **Resist Any Temptation to Use Abusive Tactics** such as sarcasm, ridicule, name-calling, or public embarrassment.

People will remember how you made them feel – good and bad – long after they forget the words. Seeing team members as they can become will help you view them in a positive light, choose the right words and actions, and encourage personal and professional growth.

....

Action I will take to help team members develop their talents:

41
HELPING TEAM MEMBERS
BECOME GOAL-DIRECTED

One of the most important motivational techniques of a successful leader is goal setting that involves all team members. Without specific goals and carefully written plans to attain them, the success of your organization is left to chance. The future of your organization is far too important to be left to chance.

It begins with you. Unless you are goal-directed and create a goal-setting climate in all levels of your organization, most of your other leadership efforts will be in vain. You can't effectively set goals for another person, but you can create a climate that encourages and develops goal-seeking attitudes. There are four basics of directing the goal setting of others:

♦ **First,** team members must choose their own goals. To accomplish any goal, people must have a genuine commitment to it. When personal goals can be realized by accomplishing organizational goals, a higher motivational climate will exist.

♦ **Second,** make it a challenge. Encourage team members to set goals and stretch themselves to do more than they have accomplished in the past. If a goal is to be motivating, some risk will be involved. Low goals don't inspire people to use their full potential and be all they can be. Goals that are set high cause people to stretch, reach, grow, and use more of their full potential. As a result, they achieve more.

♦ **Third,** establish a personal development philosophy.

When you expect your team members to grow and develop more of their talents and abilities, you can also expect and accept shortcomings. After all, if your team members already had all the qualities you possess, they would probably already be in your position or in one comparable to it. Be willing to make allowances for occasional shortcomings, and avoid being too demanding.

You will grow personally as you help your team members grow, and in effect, you will multiply yourself by building their leadership capacities. If, on the other hand, you have no tolerance for their shortcomings, you will in some form communicate this rejection to them, and they will gradually cease to set goals. The results will be the opposite of what you want to accomplish.

♦   **Fourth,** give feedback on performance. Just as you're better able to motivate yourself when you have periodic feedback on your performance, team members also need to know how they're doing. Give them frequent feedback and make it as specific as possible. In doing so, you recharge the motivating forces that originally set them on a course toward their goals.

Goal setting is a prelude to action. Goal setting is dynamic. When you and your team members set and achieve goals on a regular basis, you increase your chances of success. At the same time, team members grow, develop and begin to use more of their talents and abilities.

••

Action I will take to help team members become more goal-directed:

42
IMPROVING PERFORMANCE AND RESULTS

Performance is critical in sports, the arts, investments, business, and every area of life. To win a NASCAR event the performance of the car, driver, and pit crew are all vital to success. In team sports such as baseball, basketball, football, hockey, and soccer performance of each player and the combined team performance are crucial. In individual sports such as bowling, golf, or tennis the performance of the individual determines the results or outcome. When you spend your hard earned money to attend a concert, the performance of the artist or act is critical in determining if you had a good time and feel it was a good investment of time and money.

The way you and your teammates perform in business also determines the results you and your organization get. There are four major things that impact your ability to get results on your team:

1. Clearly defined goals

2. Attitudes

3. Skills in respective areas of responsibility

4. Your coaching ability

Assuming you have the right people in the right jobs and they have the necessary skills, the better you clarify goals, develop appropriate attitudes, and improve your coaching skills, the better your chance of improving performance and results.

Once you determine your goals, i.e. what you want to accomplish, you need to determine what performance is needed by you and your teammates to accomplish these goals. Identify what extraordinary performance would look like in specific, observable behavior terms. No one wants to be average. Therefore, when you think of performance, think of it in terms of what extraordinary performance would look like.

New goals and better results will not be achieved without improvement in individual and team performance. Extraordinary performance, outstanding utilization of skills, is mainly determined by how people think (attitude) and how they act (behavior). There is a direct correlation between the way people think and the way they act. And, there is a direct correlation between the way people act and the results they get.

You cannot necessarily "see" an attitude, but you can observe a person's behavior and make a pretty accurate assessment of his or her attitude. Yogi Berra, the Hall of Fame baseball player, is reported to have said, "You can see a lot by observing". You can learn a lot about a person's attitude by observing his or her behavior. Is the person dependable or unreliable; prompt or tardy, careful or safe; neat or sloppy; etc.

A long-term change in performance or behavior will not occur without a change in attitude. People will not change their attitude because we want them to change it or because we tell them to change it. People change three ways: slowly, rarely, and never. To accelerate the changes needed to achieve improved performance and results, you need to help people see the benefits they can gain or the losses they will avoid by changing. This takes time and it takes a concentrated effort on your part to get to know each person individually so you can personalize your coaching.

The most important coaching skill needed is the ability to help players adjust their attitude in line with the performance needed to achieve the pre-determined goals.

....

Actions I will take to improve performance and results:

43
COACHING A WINNING TEAM

Great teams have a great coaching staff, talented players, a desire for continuous improvement, a willingness of team members to help each other become more successful, and a passion for winning.

It's been said that "knowledge gets you into the game and passion wins it." Evaluate your team in these areas, especially a passion for winning – whatever winning is for your team. Determine what you need to do in order to be better.

Jim Collins, in his book, *Good to Great*, states, "Good is the enemy of great." Very few coaches become great because they settle for being "good." Knowing how to support superior performance is critical to becoming a great coach. Almost all individuals in a coaching role can substantially improve their coaching techniques and thus, their results. It is mainly a matter of conscious choice and a willingness to examine what personal behaviors need to change – for example, what behaviors do team members need to start, stop, or accelerate to achieve better results?

Listed below are 12 steps you can take to coach a winning team:

1. Be generous with encouragement.

2. Give positive feedback regarding outstanding, improved, and consistent performance.

3. Help people set and achieve personal, business, and professional development goals.

4. Communicate your expectations clearly (preferably in writing).

5. Help people clarify their thinking.

6. Reinforce the behaviors you want repeated.

7. Focus on specific issues or behaviors the person can control.

8. Avoid personal attacks, sarcasm, or innuendos.

9. Avoid inflammatory words such as should have, ought to, have to, always, and never.

10. Believe in your people.

11. Be a positive role model.

12. Stay in the moment. Give the other person your complete time and attention.

••

I will do the following to be a better coach:

44

"ENCOURAGE" CHANGE

Have you ever done anything stupid, knew at the time that it was stupid, and did it anyway? Have you ever done anything you knew was stupid, said you would never do it again, and did it again? Most, if not all of us, would have to answer "yes" to each of these questions. What does it prove? It proves we are human and we are creatures of habit.

The good news is that most habits are good because they save us time, energy, and effort. Once we turn something into a habit, the habit takes over and allows us to perform it automatically. The bad news is that the biggest threat to habit change is the habit itself. The old habit fights for its life and makes it more difficult for the new habit to take over. That is a primary reason that most people resist change; the old way is comfortable and known and the new way is threatening and scary.

If you do what you have always done, you will get what you have always gotten. If you want outcomes to be better, you need to do something different --- and that requires change. Effective leaders and coaches must expect change, encourage change, and embrace change. What worked yesterday won't necessarily work today. To meet the challenge of change, leaders must turn to their most important asset: people.

Leaders need to develop strategies for:

1. **Enhancing communication.** Growth is more likely to occur when clear communication is taking place on a regular basis.

2. **Promoting continuous learning and development.** When people learn to handle new responsibilities or develop new skills their self-confidence gets a boost and they will be capable of better performance and will accomplish more.

3. **Improving leadership skills.** Even people who do not perform a formal leadership role can improve their performance by developing leadership skills. It will also prepare them for future opportunities.

Meeting the challenge of change is easier when you use your most valuable tool: encouragement. Everyone needs and responds to encouragement. Encouragement brings out the best in people, helps people believe in themselves, and helps them accomplish more. It is amazing what people can accomplish when they believe in themselves and when the important people in their lives give them encouragement. The effective use of encouragement will work wonders and the best part is that it doesn't cost anything other than a little time and effort.

Think about someone who encouraged you and influenced your leadership ability. How is your life better because of that person? Think about people you can encourage and influence in a positive way. Then, systematically give them encouragement on a regular basis. When you do this, you will be well on your way to meeting the challenge of change.

....

Action I will take to encourage change:

45

BENEFITS OF KEEPING SCORE

♦ **Keeping score generates excitement for players and fans.** Scorekeeping improves individual and team performance; enhances concentration and focus; helps coaches and players make better decisions; helps prevent and solve problems; identifies opportunities for training; and makes it easier to accurately project outcomes.

♦ **Keeping score provides early warning signals.** The gauges on the dashboard of your vehicle provide a form of keeping score. They indicate how much fuel you have, how well your engine is performing, and whether it needs maintenance. The odometer indicates how far you have driven – overall and on a given trip. A thermostat is used to keep score on the room temperature and adjust the heat or air conditioning accordingly. In business, it is crucial to have a method of keeping score in place that provides early warning signals so you can make the appropriate adjustments.

A doctor uses a person's vital signs to keep score on how the body is performing and if any attention is needed. Scales help people know if they are maintaining their desired weight. What are the vital signs for your business? Can you identify and measure them with the same degree of accuracy as a blood pressure gauge or a set of scales?

♦ **Keeping score helps break goals into bite-sized chunks.** This promotes confidence when people think and say, "I can do that." Knowing that you are winning at small goals helps build momentum and increase your opportunities to accomplish larger goals.

♦ **Keeping score provides trends and direction.** Where you are now is important. Even more important is what direction you are moving and at what speed. Knowing trends and direction helps reduce the chance of surprises and uncertainty. Increased certainty enhances confidence and increased confidence promotes increased success.

♦ **Keeping score helps you celebrate successes.** One response to seeing the score is, "Hooray!" When you reinforce "Hooray," progress and success are reinforced. Reinforcing progress and success creates a motivational environment that leads to more progress and success.

♦ **Keeping score can help you take corrective action.** Another response to seeing the score is, "Oh no." Following "Oh no" situations with a corrective plan of action of additional training and coaching reduces future "Oh no's."

♦ **Keeping score enhances change.** Keeping score creates insight and insight precedes change. When you know where you stand and what direction you are heading, you can set new goals, adjust your behavior, and produce new or better results.

♦ **Keeping score improves accountability.** When a good scorekeeping system is in place, people can run, but they can't hide.

One day my daughter and I were playing basketball in our driveway with some of the neighborhood boys. Lindsay was nine and hadn't shown much athletic prowess yet. When the boys tired of the game, Lindsay said to me, "I'm not very good, am I dad?" Her shoulders were slumped and her chin was in her chest. I could not bear seeing her feeling bad about herself and her ability.

I said, "Sure you are", threw her the basketball and encouraged her to take more shots. After several misses, she made a basket and I said out loud, "That's one." She was startled, but continued to shoot. When she made another basket, I said, "Two", and continued to count aloud as she made additional baskets. In about 10 minutes, she had made 8 or 9 baskets. Now, her shoulders were back, her chin was up, and she said with a big smile, "I'm pretty good, ain't I dad?"

During the 10 minutes, I did not offer any shooting tips, I just kept score. Lindsay played organized basketball from the fourth grade through high school, was the leading scorer on her high school team, and made the All-District team. What a difference 10 minutes and keeping score made. Listed below are four scorekeeping principles that will help you get greater results personally and in your business when you keep score.

Keep it simple. If keeping score requires too many or complicated calculations or takes too much time, people will be reluctant to keep score. Remember the KISS principle ---

Keep It Short and Simple.

Keep it visual. A common thought is that a picture is worth a thousand words. Likewise a graph can be worth a thousand words or numerous columns of numbers. Visual scorekeeping means displaying the score prominently as well as graphically.

Keep it objective. In most sporting events, the score is rarely, if ever, in dispute. The same kind of certainty and objectivity is needed in business scorekeeping. A subjective goal such as improved communication or morale can be quantified by answering the questions, "What will be different when communication is improved?" or "… when morale is improved?" For example, there might be less mistakes, improved quality, improved attendance or improved employee retention.

You can also use the electronic scoreboard concept. If you had an electronic scoreboard at the end of your work area, what would you put on it to know that you are winning?

Keep it current. Most things in life are better when they are fresh. The same is true with scorekeeping in business. Week-old, or even day-old, numbers are not as good as 'freshly-baked," same-day numbers.

The main purpose of keeping score is to improve performance and results. Make sure you use your scorekeeping system to solve problems, not to find fault. Once problems are identified and defined, use the insight you gain from keeping score to decide what corrective action is needed.

Computers have given business leaders better access and

more information to operate their businesses. When you use this information to keep score, you can make remarkable improvements in performance and results.

....

Areas in which I'll do a better job of keeping score:

INSIGHT PRECEDES CHANGE

Championship athletes and teams keep statistics to improve performance and results. In basketball, statistics include shooting percentage (field goals, 3 point and free throws), rebounds, steals, assists, and turnovers. In baseball, it is batting averages, earned runs averages, slugging percentage, on-base percentage, stolen bases, walks, strikeouts, and fielding average. Similar categories exist in every sport.

Unfortunately, in business, too many people think they are too busy "working" to keep statistics. When you keep track of the appropriate statistics and monitor them on a frequent basis, you can work smarter instead of harder and you will have more time for important tasks.

A manufacturing company had a horrendous absenteeism problem. It was costing them a lot of money in overtime and temporary services. Mistakes were being made and they were losing customers. Management tried everything they could think of to correct the problem, but without success. During a management development process, the problem surfaced and the facilitator asked some insightful questions that produced some startling results.

His questions involved who, what, when, where, how, and why. When he got to "When is it occurring?" the answer was "We don't know." And he said, "Let's find out." The team gathered statistics from the previous six months and presented them several different ways. When they looked at the per day statistics, the insight paid off. They found that Monday through Thursday attendance was in an acceptable range, but Friday attendance missed the mark drastically.

When the managers were asked why they thought this was happening, they said it was probably because they paid people on Thursdays. When asked why they did that, the classic response was because we've always done it that way. When asked what would happen if they changed payday to Fridays, the response was "We don't know." The facilitator said, "Let's find out." They changed payday to Fridays and their absenteeism problem shrunk to an acceptable size. The benefits were substantial. Without the insight, the problem would probably still exist today, or worse yet, they would be out of business.

Do you have lingering problems that you have not been able to solve or goals you have been unable to reach? Take a new look at statistics that are available to you and/or set up a scorekeeping system to get new statistics. Electronic spreadsheets are a great way to look at a set of statistics in many different ways so you can gain additional insight. Ask questions starting with who, what, when, where, how, and why to identify opportunities for improvement.

48
JUST FOR TODAY

Sometimes it can seem daunting to exchange one attitude or behavior for a better one. However, if you focus on what you can do one day at a time for several days, the new attitude or behavior will be firmly entrenched. Here are 30 suggestions to get you started. Feel free to adopt any or all of these and some of your own:

1. Encourage someone.

2. Treat everyone you meet with dignity and respect.

3. Complete an action step for one of your goals.

4. Listen more than you talk.

5. Ask better questions.

6. Focus on your strengths.

7. Look for the good in people.

8. Help people be right.

9. Keep people informed.

10. Avoid email "gun battles."

11. Avoid getting angry.

12. Help someone feel important or special.

13. Send someone a hand-written note or letter.

14. Read 10 pages of a personal improvement book.

15. Spend quality time with a family member and/or

colleague.

16. Start a new project.

17. Complete an unfinished project.

18. Catch people doing things right (or almost right).

19. Avoid using personal attacks, sarcasm, or innuendos when disciplining someone.

20. Delegate something that the other person can do better, faster, at less cost, or can use as a training opportunity.

21. Avoid interrupting people or finishing their sentences.

22. Perform an act of kindness for a customer or colleague.

23. Ask the magic question, "What do you think?"

24. Try to learn something from everyone you meet.

25. Learn something new about one of your team members.

26. Make the magic statement, "Tell me about it" when someone is upset or is presenting a problem.

27. Look at how things can be done instead of why they can't be done.

28. Do not say anything about anyone that you wouldn't say to his or her face.

29. Show appreciation to someone.

30. Communicate more than you think is necessary and, in most cases, it will probably be just right.

49

LIVING AND LEADING WITH
A POSITIVE OUTLOOK

Learning to deal with problems and difficulties is a major concern of leaders, managers, sales professionals, parents, and friends. A key factor in living and leading with a positive outlook is emotional stability. By learning to deal with each problem or difficulty in one of three ways, you can maintain emotional stability:

1. Through good management of yourself and others, you prevent many problems.

2. Through exercising your problem-solving skills, you learn to solve problems as they arise and avoid emotional reactions to the surrounding circumstances.

3. Through practical reasoning and a positive mental attitude, you can choose to endure unwanted events and problem situations that can be neither avoided nor changed and can even learn to turn them into profit. In other words, "turn lemons into lemonade."

Emotional calm is a direct result of what goes on inside - a result of reactions to events and circumstances according to one's opinions and judgments. You're conditioned to respond in certain ways based on family influences, social environment, education, and past mistakes and failures. Your response to what happens to you is usually, if not always, more important than what actually happens.

You have an experience whenever something happens to you or around you. When you recognize dissatisfaction with the experience and feel uneasiness, pain, or physical or mental distress, you begin thinking of a way to handle the situation that will satisfy your wants and expectations. You either, arrive at a satisfactory opinion through your thinking and finally see nothing to be disturbed about, or else become emotionally upset. On the positive side, you decide what to do and how to do it in order to solve the problem or to make a satisfactory adjustment to what's going on. Then you feel confident that the matter can be dealt with effectively. You can take deliberate action in line with your decision and dispose of the matter without emotional distress.

We have all experienced the negative side of this process. Until you arrive at a satisfactory opinion, idea, or understanding, you can't decide what to do. As a result, you experience feelings of fear, confusion, or anxiety. You can't see a satisfactory way out of the situation. Irritation, resentment, or anger follows, and you either fight or run away from the situation. A manifestation of this can be seen in what is called "road rage." Without an understanding, you can't see a way to protect yourself or to achieve your purpose, because you can neither adjust yourself to the circumstances nor change your emotional reactions to them.

A goal to deal with negative emotions is consistent with the goal of achieving harmony, good will, and cooperation from others. Becoming angry and condemning people causes them to lose confidence in you and sets up obstacles against achieving cooperation with them. The first step in improving your level of confidence as a leader, manager, sales professional, parent, or friend is to change the way you think about events and people. When you can arrive at opinions and judgments without experiencing anger or negative feelings toward others, you can attain the confidence of others. Good intentions or resolutions about not becoming angry will never work, but living and leading with a positive outlook will.

....

Actions I will take to live and lead with a more positive outlook:

50
MAINTAINING JOB SATISFACTION

Job satisfaction, or dissatisfaction, is one of the greatest indicators of the motivational environment or morale of an organization. Each team member has needs that must be satisfied. An effective leader will identify these personal needs and help the employee translate them into personal goals. Then, help the team member see how these personal goals will help the organization achieve its goals.

Because all team members are people, and therefore reflect different heritages, environments, and training, there is no single method or idea that will successfully motivate all of them at all times.

However, within the context of motivational leadership (leadership through a stimulating climate of motivation), the leader can maintain an atmosphere that is conducive to personal motivation, job satisfaction, and individual growth. The leader can create a motivational environment that will allow for increased individual, team success, and job satisfaction.

As a leader, it is your responsibility to create a climate for growth and learn to deal with each of your team member's motivational needs on an individual basis.

To do this, you need to be observant, spend one-on-one time with each team member, ask questions, listen, and genuinely care about each team member.

Leading by example is one of the best ways to accomplish the above. Listed below are some ideas that will help you lead by example. These ideas are excerpted from the book, *Awakening Corporate Soul: Four Paths to Unleash the Power of People at Work* by Eric Klein & Dr. John Izzo - www.theizzogroup.com and www.dharmaconsulting.com.

1. Take responsibility for loving your job instead of blaming others.

2. Focus on what you are passionate about in your job.

3. Avoid sarcasm.

4. Make a list of things you are thankful for in your work.

5. Set work and learning goals, for yourself, for your team.

6. Become more creative in your work.

7. Balance your work with important outside activities.

8. Perform one act of kindness for your customers or colleagues every day.

9. Review and renew job resolutions regularly.

••

Action I will take to unleash the power of people in our work group:

51
HOW TO KEEP YOUR
GOALS PROGRAM ALIVE

Set low goals and raise them gradually. This creates a sense of winning which will boost your self-confidence, self-image, self-esteem, and enthusiasm for new and larger goals.

Break larger goals into bite-size chunks. Larger goals can be both motivating and overwhelming at the same time. Breaking them into smaller goals will create motivation without overwhelming you.

Keep score. What gets measured, tracked, and reported gets done. The way you keep score can be as simple as hash marks, a barometer, a graph, or other symbols. The keys to effective scorekeeping are to keep it simple, visual, and dynamic.

Schedule action steps in specific time slots or days. When you put things on your calendar, in specific time slots, you are more likely to act on them.

Set priorities. Determine what is most important and tackle the most important action steps first.

Make public commitments. Let people who support you and your goals know what your goals are and what you are doing, or have done, to achieve them. This will help you hold yourself accountable.

Ask for help if you need it. In the same vein that you miss 100 percent of the shots you don't take, you are not going to get much help with your goals unless you ask for it. An early mentor of mine told me that successful people are willing to ask for help.

Use affirmations to support your goals. An affirmation is a positive declaration stated as if it were true. Affirmations are tools to help you achieve a goal. They are not true or false. Your subconscious mind cannot tell the difference between fact and fantasy. It believes anything it is told. It is also a servomechanism that guides your thoughts and behaviors. You can program your subconscious mind to develop the thoughts and behaviors necessary for the accomplishment of your goals by using affirmations.

Affirmations need to be written and read daily or memorized and recited daily. For best results, use the personal pronoun "I" and state your affirmations positively and in the present tense. Using the personal pronoun "I" addresses your subconscious mind.

Stating your affirmations positively is important because your mind grasps positives better than negatives. For example, if you want to adjust your weight, it is better to say, "I weigh 160 pounds" rather than "I will lose 20 pounds." Or, another example is, "I am enjoying record-setting consecutive safe days" rather than "I don't want anyone to get hurt."

Using the present tense takes advantage of the "act as if" principle. The subconscious mind responds well to positive, action-oriented commands. If you want to be happy, act happy; if you want to be enthusiastic, act enthusiastic; if you want to be energetic, act energetic.

Use visualization to support your goals. Put pictures that symbolize your goal when it is accomplished in prominent places such as your desk, your bathroom mirror, your refrigerator, the dash or visor of your car, and/or any other place where you will see it regularly. You can also create a "visualization board" out of poster board or cork board, and place it where you will see it regularly.

In a 1970s TV show, Flip Wilson's character, Geraldine, said, "What you see is what you get." The same is true about your goals when you visualize them. The passenger side mirror on your car has a statement etched on the bottom portion that says: "Objects in mirror are closer than they appear." The accomplishment of your goals will be closer than they appear when you use good visualization techniques.

••

Actions I will take to keep my goals program alive:

52

MANAGEMENT RESOLUTIONS FOR THE NEW YEAR - II

THROUGHOUT THE NEW YEAR I WILL:

1. Work from a written and specific goals program and make mid-course corrections as needed to achieve my important personal and professional goals.

2. Work to improve all my personal and professional relationships by listening to understand, staying in the moment, and by being trustworthy.

3. Make every person I interact with feel important by treating them with dignity and respect.

4. Make sure each person understands his or her specific role in making the team a success.

5. Eliminate common timewasters and stay in high payoff activities.

6. Teach others how to do more, how to do it better, and how to come closer and closer to their full potential.

7. Learn from others as well as from books, CDs, and seminars.

8. Focus on what I can control and not waste time on things I can't control.

9. Get individuals to mesh their goals with team goals.

10. Pay attention, listen, and learn.

11. Be optimistic and enthusiastic.

12. Always be prepared.

13. Lead by example.

14. Develop a high sense of urgency for outcomes.

15. Be patient with people, especially when they are being trained or learning something new.

16. Accept personal responsibility and hold team members accountable.

17. Act quickly to correct inappropriate behavior in a positive manner.

18. Look for ways to show appreciation and show my appreciation often.

HAPPY PRODUCTIVE & PROFITABLE NEW YEAR!

I will be better in the new year in the following ways:

In order to make a difference in your own life and in the lives of those around you, you must apply the ideas and behaviors you read about within this book.

As you apply these behaviors, take the time to recognize the changes in both yourself and those around you. Recognition will enhance motivation and motivation will ensure greater success.

Since reading this book, I have made the following changes:

AFTERWORD

A young man learns what's most important in life from the guy next door.

It had been some time since Jack had seen the old man. College, girls, career, and life itself got in the way. In fact, Jack moved clear across the country in pursuit of his dreams. There, in the rush of his busy life, Jack had little time to think about the past and often no time to spend with his wife and son. He was working on his future, and nothing could stop him.

Over the phone, his mother told him, "Mr. Belser died last night. The funeral is Wednesday." Memories flashed through his mind like an old newsreel as he sat quietly remembering his childhood days.

"Jack, did you hear me?"

"Oh, sorry, Mom. Yes, I heard you. It's been so long since I thought of him. I'm sorry, but I honestly thought he died years ago," Jack said.

"Well, he didn't forget you. Every time I saw him he'd ask how you were doing. He'd reminisce about the many days you spent over 'his side of the fence' as he put it," Mom told him.

"I loved that old house he lived in," Jack said.

"You know, Jack, after your father died, Mr. Belser stepped in to make sure you had a man's influence in your life," she said.

"He's the one who taught me carpentry," he said. "I wouldn't be in this business if it weren't for him. He spent a lot of time teaching me things he thought were important... Mom, I'll be there for the funeral," Jack said.

As busy as he was, he kept his word. Jack caught the next flight to his hometown. Mr. Belser's funeral was small and uneventful. He had no children of his own, and most of his relatives had passed away.

The night before he had to return home, Jack and his Mom stopped by to see the old house next door one more time. Standing in the doorway, Jack paused for a moment. It was like crossing over into another dimension, a leap through space and time. The house was exactly as he remembered. Every step held memories; every picture, every piece of furniture. Jack stopped suddenly.

"What's wrong, Jack?" his Mom asked. "The box is gone," he said. "What box?" his Mom asked.

"There was a small gold box that he kept locked on top of his desk. I must have asked him a thousand times what was inside. All he'd ever tell me was 'the thing I value most,'" Jack said.

It was gone. Everything about the house was exactly how Jack remembered it, except for the box. He figured someone from the Belser family had taken it.

"Now I'll never know what was so valuable to him," Jack said. "I better get some sleep. I have an early flight home, Mom."

It had been about two weeks since Mr. Belser died. Returning home from work one day Jack discovered a note in his mailbox. "Signature required on a package. No one at home. Please stop by the main post office within the next three days," the note read.

Early the next day Jack retrieved the package. The small box was old and looked like it had been mailed a hundred years ago. The handwriting was difficult to read, but the return address caught his attention.

"Mr. Harold Belser" it read. Jack took the box out to his car and ripped open the package. There inside was the gold box and an envelope. Jack's hands shook as he read the note inside.

"Upon my death, please forward this box and its contents to Jack Bennett. It's the thing I valued most in my life."

A small key was taped to the letter. His heart racing, as tears filling his eyes, Jack carefully unlocked the box. There inside he found a beautiful gold pocket watch. Running his fingers slowly over the finely etched casing, he unlatched the cover.

Inside he found these words engraved: "Jack, Thanks for your time! Harold Belser." "The thing he valued most...was my time."

Jack held the watch for a few minutes, then called his office and cleared is appointments for the next two days.

"Why?" Janet, his assistant asked. "I need some time to spend with my son," he said. "Oh, by the way, Janet...thanks for your time!"

"Life is not measured by the number of breaths we take but by the moments that take our breath away,"

Thank you for your time.....

- Author Unknown

Do more than exist: *LIVE*
Do more than touch: *FEEL*
Do more than look: *OBSERVE*
Do more than read: *ABSORB*
Do more than hear: *LISTEN*
Do more than listen: *UNDERSTAND*
Do more than think: *REFLECT*
Do more than just talk: *SAY SOMETHING*

MAKING A DIFFERENCE

Have you ever stopped to wonder about the opportunity you have to make a difference in your own life and in the lives of those around you?

You can help someone or hurt them; unleash someone's potential or squash it; motivate someone or de-motivate them; build someone up or tear them down; learn how to bring out the best in someone or settle for sub-standard performance; encourage or discourage someone.

Every person has the ability to make a difference. Some will employ their ability, while others will ignore it.

The books in the MAKING A DIFFERENCE series provide readers with valuable information that will make a difference by bringing out the best in themselves and others. The ultimate goal is to improve performance and results.

The topics are relevant to individuals in every industry, regardless of position or experience. Each book is easy to read, and the ideas can be implemented immediately.

To learn more about improving your performance and results or the performance and results of others, or for more information on additional products, we encourage you to visit our website at:

www.improve-results.com

Or, call us toll free at 1-866-370-3509.

Improving
Performance
&Results

Making a Difference

ABOUT THE AUTHOR

Rex Houze has been helping business leaders improve their performance, results, and quality of life since 1972.

He is an accomplished speaker, workshop leader, facilitator, and businessman. His fast-paced, enthusiastic style captivates audiences and makes learning and participating fun. He is the founder and CEO of Improving Performance & Results, Inc., a company dedicated to helping leaders in business bring out the best in people.

Rex's unique ability to communicate clearly, simply, and precisely has made him a much sought-after speaker and communicator who has conducted speeches and workshops for hundreds of groups throughout the United States, Canada, Mexico, Australia, and New Zealand.

In addition to speaking, Rex is the author of three leadership development and productivity improvement programs: *Coaching for Improved Performance & Results, Improving Performance & Results,* and *Getting Results Through Others.*

He has also authored two self-improvement booklets: *What a Difference TEN Minutes Can Make* and *Getting Better Results.*

He is also the co-author of *Bridging the Leadership Gap.*

Rex's continual commitment to help leaders bring out the best in themselves and others prompted the creation of *LEADERSHIP INSIGHTS.*

Questions and comments about *LEADERSHIP INSIGHTS* are encouraged and may be sent to :
r.houze@sbcglobal.net or 1-866-370-3509

Index

Solitary confinement 98
Stone, W. Clement 29, 63
Strengths 20, 38, 51, 53, 82–83,
        86, 100, 114
Success 56, 86, 106
    12 steps 52–54
Successes 79, 126
Synergy 38, 43, 61

T

Team 74, 94, 95, 106–107,
        121–122
    effectiveness 43–44
    members 41, 82–84, 102,
        113–115, 116–117, 137
    morale 47–49
    productivity 45–46
Teamwork 44, 49, 95
The One Minute Manager® 31
The Power of Full Engagement
        81
Thurber, James 27
Timewasters 34–35
Trust 40–42, 65, 75, 92

U

Uncertainty 41, 48, 80

V

Vision 62–63, 65–66
Visualization 140–141
Visualization board 141

W

Walton, Sam 30
Watt, Ron 67
Weaknesses 20, 51, 53, 82–84
Whittier, John G. 31
Win/win attitude. *See* attitude
Winning 58–59

team 121–122
Wisdom 27
Wooden, John 31, 58
Work habits 106

Y

Your Greatest Power 17, 56

If you enjoyed *LEADERSHIP INSIGHTS*, we encourage you to subscribe to our monthly electronic newsletter. Each issue contains a new leadership insight. And, its FREE. You can subscribe at www.improve-results.com by clicking on FREE SUBSCRIPTIONS and following the instructions.

We also encourage you to call us about quantity discounts for *LEADERSHIP INSIGHTS* so you can:

- Give a copy to each of your managers and/or all of your employees (you can review an insight a week)
- Provide as gifts to your key clients
- Donate copies to the Leadership organization in your city

Other products we have available include:

Comprehensive programs*

- ❏ *Improving Performance & Results*
- ❏ *Coaching for Improved Performance & Results*
- ❏ *Getting Results Through Others*

*These programs can be implemented by one of our professional facilitators or you can engage us to certify one or more people from your organization to implement any or all of them.

Booklets

- ❏ *What a Difference TEN Minutes Can Make*
- ❏ *Getting Better Results, 101 Quick Tips for Personal and Organizational Success*

Audio CDs

- ❏ *Keeping Score to WIN*
- ❏ *The Art of Asking Questions*

- *Bridging the Leadership Gap (also available on DVD)*
- *Mastering Intentional Communication*
- *Manage Yourself, Not Time*
- *Effective Feedback*
- *Goal Setting for Success*

For more information or to order any of the products listed, visit our website at **www.improve-results.com** or call us at **866-370-3509.**

BONUS THOUGHT

The dreams we dream can be fulfilled,
If when we dream, we also build.
And we can build the dreams we choose,
Depending on the tools we use.
If we would build to greater heights,
We have to raise our hopes and sights.
When hopes and sights are only small,
We can't build lofty, high, and tall.
Thoughts must be big for big success,
Why be content with something less.
Sights must be high if we'd build high,
But, faith has wings, so why not fly.
To see your hopes and dreams come true,
Think big, think high, think good, think new.
The years can see them all fulfilled,
By how you think and how you build.

- Author Unknown

LEADERSHIP INSIGHTS ORDER FORM

Give the priceless gift of leadership ideas to all those in your network.

❑ Yes, I want _____ copies of *Leadership Insights* at $19.95 each, plus $4 shipping for the first book and $2 shipping for each additional book (Texas residents add $1.65 sales tax per book). Quantity pricing available upon request.

❑ My check or money order for $_____ is enclosed.

❑ Please charge my
    ❑ Visa   ❑ Mastercard   ❑ American Express

International orders must be paid by credit card or by postal money order in U.S. funds. Please add $6 shipping per book.

Name _____

Organization _____

Address _____

City/Sate/Zip _____

Phone _____ Email _____

Card # _____ Exp Date _____

Signature _____

❑ Yes, I would like to receive a FREE subscription to Leadership Insights electronic tips.

Please make check or money order payable to:

Improving Performance & Results, Inc.
425 Stone Bridge Circle
Allen, TX 75013

Order online at www.improve-results.com

Or email at r.houze@sbcglobal.net

Or by phone at 1-866-370-3509

Or by fax at 1-214-509-0082